MOTHER *of* PEARL

luminous lessons and iridescent faith

compiled by MARGARET MCSWEENEY

Inspiring Voices®
A Service of **Guideposts**

Inspiring Voices books may be ordered through booksellers or by contacting:

Inspiring Voices
1663 Liberty Drive
Bloomington, IN 47403
www.inspiringvoices.com
1-(866) 697-5313

Because of the dynamic nature of the Internet, any web addresses or links contained in this book may have changed since publication and may no longer be valid. The views expressed in this work are solely those of the author and do not necessarily reflect the views of the publisher, and the publisher hereby disclaims any responsibility for them.

Certain stock imagery © Thinkstock.
Any people depicted in stock imagery provided by Thinkstock are models, and such images are being used for illustrative purposes only.

ISBN: 978-1-4624-0159-8 (e)
ISBN: 978-1-4624-0158-1 (sc)

Library of Congress Control Number: 2012938426

Printed in the United States of America

Inspiring Voices rev. date: 5/8/2012

Margaret McSweeney has created another collection that will warm your heart and touch your life. Offering personal encouragement from a variety of women (many whose names you'll recognize), this book is a treasure chest you can return to again and again. It holds blessings for you personally and all the mothers in your life as well.

—**HOLLEY GERTH,** author of *You're Already Amazing*

Contents

A NOTE FROM MARGARET
ABOUT PEARL GIRLS®

Like the oyster, women encounter unexpected grit during our everyday lives. However, God's nacre of love and grace covers our grit and transforms the pain into a precious pearl. Nothing is ever beyond God's grace. How fitting that nacre, also known as Mother of Pearl, leaves a layered, luminous lining within a shell. This brilliant luster is strong, lasting and purposeful – just like the love, lessons and legacies that are left by the special women in our lives. These heartprints that can help guide and comfort us even when our mothers are no longer with us.

My mother passed away nearly a decade ago when I was 41. I loved my mother; and I regret that we never shared the close bond that I always had with my gregarious dad. My dad was the effusive encourager and optimist who lived his faith in God like an action verb. My mother was a gentle and kind person who deeply loved her family and the Lord, and she led a life of quiet faith writing many Christian books. My dad's lustrous life in many ways eclipsed the silent radiance of my mother's layered lessons of faith, hope and love. Just recently, while writing *Aftermath: Finding Grace through Grief*, I at last discovered the treasure of my mother's individual iridescence. Through my mother's love letters to my dad, her letters to me (some mailed and some never mailed), her private journal entries, her published books and even videos never seen, I got to know the essence of who she was as a person, a wife, a Christian, a friend, a daughter and yes, even as a mother. She was my true Mother of Pearl.

This book is a compilation and celebration of women who were and are a mother of pearl. May the lustrous stories written by some of your favorite authors bless you, strengthen you and remind you always of God's iridescent grace.

The purpose of Pearl Girls® is two-fold: 1) Connecting with each other online and in-person; and 2) Collaborating on projects for charity. Linked together as a community of women who share a love for God, the Pearl Girls® reach out to help other women and children who are having a difficult time.

By purchasing a copy of *Mother of Pearl*, you, too are making a tangible impact on the lives of others. All proceeds go in full to these charities and projects:

- **Wings (Women in Need Growing Stronger)** www. wingsprogram.com Located in a Chicago suburb, this non-profit organization provides a Safe House and transitional homes and services for women and their children who are fleeing from domestic violence. Half of the proceeds from *Mother of Pearl* will go directly to help hire a manager for the Safe House. This "Safe House Mother" will be a source of comfort and encouragement for the women and children who seek safe shelter through Wings.
- **Hands of Hope** www.handsofhopeonline.org This charity helps women and children in Africa. Half of the proceeds from *Mother of Pearl* will go directly to help build a well for school children in Zambia.

Thank you for becoming one of the Pearl Girls.®
Please visit the Pearl Girls® website www.pearlgirls.info
to connect and share your own story.

Christmas Without Grandma Kay

"Okay," I agreed with my husband. "We'll invite your family for Christmas. But you know how hard it's going to be since your mom passed away."

"I know," Ross said. "That's why we all need to be together."

I braced myself for a holiday punctuated by sorrow.

On Christmas Eve, the adults settled in the living room and Ross began our family tradition of reading from Luke 2. At verse eight, our six-year-old, Rachel, appeared at the top of the stairs wearing her brother's bathrobe and carrying a stuffed lamb under her arm.

Next came my niece, donning an old blue robe. Her hands supported the plastic baby doll bundled at her middle. My son, appearing as Joseph, discreetly turned his head away as Mary "brought forth" her firstborn, wrapped him in a dish towel and laid him in the laundry basket.

Ross turned to Matthew 2 and read the cue for the Magi. "We saw his star in the east and have come to worship him."

One of my nephews whispered, "You go first!" and pushed his older brother out of the bedroom into full view. Slowly, the ultimate wise guy descended with Rachel's black tutu on his head and bearing a large bottle of canola oil.

The adults burst out laughing. I did too, until I realized what he was wearing. My father-in-law recognized the kimono style dress too

1

and said, "Hey! That's Kay's dress! What are you doing wearing her dress?"

I cringed, wishing the kids hadn't gotten into my closet. They had found the bags I'd stored there last summer, hoping for a day by myself when I could reverently sort through the last of Kay's belongings. The clothes and scarfs in those bags still carried the faint scent of her perfume.

Rachel looked at Grandpa from her perch at the top of the staircase. "Grandma doesn't mind if he uses it," she said. "I know she doesn't."

We all glanced at each other, waiting for Grandpa's reaction.

I didn't doubt that Rachel had an inside track into her grandma's heart. Earlier that year, when Kay had unexpectedly gone into a diabetic coma, Ross flew to the hospital while the children and I stayed home and prayed it would only be a close call. But one night that week, Rachel couldn't sleep. She had to talk to Grandma Kay.

I called the hospital and asked for Kay's room. Ross answered at her bedside and explained to Rachel that she would have to speak loudly because of the noisy machines that were helping Grandma breathe.

"Grandma, it's me, Rachel!" she shouted. "I wanted to tell you good night. And I'll see you in heaven."

Rachel handed me the phone and nestled down under the covers. "Oh!" She sprang back up. "Tell Daddy to give Grandma three squeezes for me."

It was Grandma Kay who taught Rachel that a silent squeeze-squeeze-squeeze of the hand means "I-love-you." I had felt those three squeezes many times, including the day after Rachel was born. Grandma Kay had flown across two states and arrived at the hospital with two pink roses grown in her garden and three warm squeezes grown in her heart.

A week after Grandma Kay's passing our extended family boarded a chartered yacht at Newport Beach. She loved her kitchen window view of the ocean and had left clear instructions that she wanted to be cremated and her ashes scattered over the Pacific. Earlier that afternoon, with a dozen memorial flower arrangements around the house, Rachel had secretly instructed her cousins to "pick a bouquet for Grandma, to take on the boat."

It was a painfully gorgeous summer evening. Saying goodbye as the sun lowered itself into the deep blue was much sweeter than huddling together to watch a sealed box lowered into the dark earth.

Once the yacht was out to sea, Rachel and her cousins tossed their hand-picked bouquets on the water. I was caught by surprise when I saw that Rachel's bouquet was centered with two pink roses. She truly had a heart connection with her grandma.

Now, Christmas Eve, in our snow-covered house, it was Rachel who welcomed Grandma Kay's memory into our celebration as she pleaded with Grandpa a second time. "Grandma wouldn't mind if we used her dress. She would like it."

Grandpa nodded, and the pageant continued. A sense of comfort quietly settled on the room. Instead of the shawl of invisible sorrow I'd expected, we were all strangely cheered by our own private memories of a woman who had loved each of us with generosity and grace.

My heart melted and I gave way to tears that I had not yet been able to shed. Rachel came down the stairs and sat beside me. Her small hand nuzzled its way into mine and she gave me three silent squeezes.

ROBIN JONES GUNN is the much-loved author of Peculiar Treasures, On a Whim, and the Christy Miller, Sierra Jensen, College Years, Glenbrooke, and Sisterchicks series, with over 4 million books sold worldwide. Robin loves to travel and often speaks locally and internationally. Visit Robin's website at www.robingunn.com.

3

An Ode to Mothers and Daughters

The journey began with one final, gigantic push, one indignant yowl, and then one triumphant shout: "It's a girl!" A moment later that precious baby was in my arms, and I reveled in the high of my life. I am that mother. Susan, now grown, is my daughter.

One early California morning, Susan called me from her home in the Midwest. "Mom, will you write a book with me about hospice?" Her request was not a total surprise. After all, this was the daughter who, on her tenth birthday, announced that she intended to open a babysitting business. When I questioned her readiness to bottle-feed infants, she responded with the utmost confidence, "Hmmph. All you need to do is milk 'em." That same self-assurance echoed in her latest plan.

Actually, I understood my daughter's passion for hospice work. Both of us were active hospice volunteers. We also share a common background as registered nurses. I reach back to the nursing profession's Stone Age, when we bandaged head injuries with medicinal poultices and hoped for the best. Later, I became a clinical psychologist and an author. As for Susan, she remained on the cutting edge of the nursing profession while attending law school. Soon, hospice became her sole professional pursuit.

"Send me your stories." I knew I was hooked.

Over the years, Susan had collected stories from hospice professionals including nurses, aides, and doctors, as well as patients and family members. Those stories made it clear that we were to write a simple, friendly, honest, compassionate work designed to help anyone learn about excellent end-of-life care. Using patients' words, we related sad, inspiring, and sometimes humorous stories of how real people deal with death and dying, and the profound difference hospice can make in reaching a peaceful, dignified death.

Working together as mother and daughter *and* colleagues was pure joy. Our family values of mutual respect and courteous disagreement were already in place, as was a solid foundation of love, trust, and deep appreciation for our different yet complementary skills. We worked as equals: no big, bossy mamma from me, and no sassy, delayed adolescence from Susan. When there was a difference of opinion we talked it out and relied upon facts over opinions. We developed an unspoken understanding: each of us would contribute our finest effort and help the other to do the same.

Over the next year, we telephoned or emailed almost daily. We studied new research findings and reports of current medical practices. Mostly, my job was to edit and defer to Susan's comprehensive knowledge of hospice. In turn, she welcomed my professional insights about some extraordinary behaviors and intense emotions that surround the dying process.

Looking back on the journey of the book, I can appreciate another story--a love story of a mother and daughter who stepped out of traditional roles and came together in a twenty-first century relationship. We created a work to help bring peace and reduce suffering during life's most challenging passage.

Our journeys continue. Currently Susan Riker Dolan is Director of Angels Grace Hospice, located in the south suburbs of Chicago, which enables her to live her dream of providing excellent end-of-life care. I write and read and continue to feel profound gratitude for that moment when I cried, "It's a girl!"

AUDREY RIKER VIZZARD, RN EDD, is a registered nurse and clinical psychologist. She is a former adjunct professor of psychology at Purdue University, and the author of many book and articles. She and her daughter, Susan Riker Dolan, are the authors of The End of Life Advisor: Personal, Legal, and Medical Considerations for a Peaceful, Dignified Death, published by Kaplan.

Bigger and Better Than a Love of Books

Today when I dropped off my son at preschool, his teacher gave me the latest order form from Scholastic Books. I'm a little sheepish to admit I reacted to the colorful pages of newsprint the same way I did when I was his age. Thirty-five years ago, I'd use my mother's pen to circle all the books that interested me (about seventy-five percent of the selections) and then negotiate with her for the actual purchase. She always bought at least one.

I have many vivid preschool memories of waking on mild California mornings, shuffling down the hall in search of Mom, and finding her reading her Bible in the dawning sunlight of the living-room window.

Before she became a Christian, my mother was a voracious reader of novels, memoir, and history. After her conversion, she feared she had wasted too many precious hours on literary escape and went on something of a book fast, a Lenten-type season of turning away from any volume that didn't deepen her understanding of Scripture. It was a profitable self-discipline that rooted her quickly in the faith. I also believe the exercise gave her permission to return to her beloved pastime afterward, albeit with a new perspective.

Back then I was too young to appreciate the love of a mother who didn't superimpose her own life journey on her children. During her own "fast" from books, she didn't starve us of good stories.

Together Mom and I read *Are You My Mother?* over and over until at age three I memorized it, *Mike Mulligan's Steam Shovel, Where the Wild Things Are,* and *The Little House.* We read Beverly Cleary and E. B. White and C. S. Lewis and Roald Dahl. Even after I was reading on my own, she gifted me with my own set of the historical Laura Ingalls Wilder, the mysterious Nancy Drew, the romantic Frances Hodgson Burnett, the biblical Marjorie Holmes and Ellen Gunderson Traylor.

And then, after my love of reading was firmly established, she recognized my interest in writing and supported that with equal devotion.

"Why don't you write that good idea down?" she would often say to me. She nudged me to write poetry for gifts and short stories for the fun of it. She copied these and passed them around to relatives.

I belong to a mother who believes that God places gifts within our hearts to bring Him and others joy, and we should pursue these loves without apology. Today she is the first person to read the first drafts of the books *I* write.

I love books because I associate them so closely with my mother's love. I crack a book and think of sitting with her as a child, pressed up against her Cristalle-scented body. I think of perusing bookstore shelves for long afternoons, knowing she was just an aisle or two away. I think of coming home from college and talking with her about the books I was reading in lit class. (We both read all of Chaim Potok's books during those years.) I think of meeting at a coffee shop and showing off new poetry acquisitions, talking about where we learned of them and what we think so far.

I don't know if my own love of books will rub off on either of my children. One of them is, in adolescence, a self-declared non-reader. But that's not the point, is it? The point is not that my children's journeys will follow mine, that they will love everything that I love. More than a love of books, my mother passed on to me a love of helping a child unearth God's gifts and embrace them.

Today, I watch my own kids' gifts emerge. Some are like mine and some are not. Both are cause for shared joy. Both are morphing and maturing in these young exciting lives. I can't wait to see what they will become.

And in the meantime, because my children are still officially children, I think I'll go fill out that book-club order form and add a few more titles to our burgeoning bookshelves.

· · · · · · · · · · · · · · · · · · · ·

ERIN HEALY and her son spend many evenings together reading their Scholastic purchases, most recently the tongue-twisting, mouth-busting Skippyjon Jones. And though her teen daughter doesn't like to read, she has listened to the audio editions of all of Erin's supernatural suspense titles, which include The Baker's Wife and House of Mercy. She lives with these great kids and their dad in Colorado Springs. For more information about Erin, please visit www.erinhealy.com.

I encourage you to learn to recognize and honor your children's unique gifts by giving them the opportunities to explore them. Even gifts that are different from yours might become something you can hold in common just because you take an interest.

A Life to Emulate

Mary Domitella Colburn. Not a household name by any stretch of the imagination. The ninety years my grandmother lived on this earth were simply not enough, although the lessons she taught could fill an entire volume of encyclopedias. Her legacy is the people whose lives she touched—and there were plenty.

My grandparents lived a modest life, but they wanted for nothing. They were blessed and they shared their blessings with everyone. Their biggest blessings came in relationships. They invested time in everyone.

Growing up, grandma's lap was always the place to be. I would run into her house, go into the kitchen, find grandma and jump in her lap. It was perfect for snuggling. It was safe. It was always good to get that reassuring hug and kiss and know that life was good.

My grandma was all about people. Nothing was more important than engaging in relationships. I always was going with grandma to visit friends. We were forever bringing someone bakery goods and helping in one way or another. Service to others was instilled at a very young age, but it wasn't talked about, it was just done. My grandparents didn't wait to be asked to help; they just knew what was needed because they took time to care about what was happening in the lives of those around them.

Family gatherings were a big part of my childhood. They were huge, chaotic and loud. People were everywhere with enough food for a small country. We had first, second, probably even fourth cousins twice removed. It didn't matter who you were. If you were important to someone Grandma loved (and Grandma loved everyone) you were invited, welcomed, and made one of the family. It was so much more than a party. It was building community. It taught me even as a young child that I belonged to something much bigger than my five-person family.

It built my self-esteem, showing me I mattered, I was loved, and that we belonged together. I took it for granted at the time, but I realize now these gatherings were as unique as they were sacred.

Every day I pray I can give my children the sense of family; of the knowledge that, although we may not be rich by the world standards, we are most certainly wealthy.

The most important thing about Grandma was her faith. It was the only thing in her life she did quietly. She spoke her mind daily, but her actions showed her faith. Yet that doesn't mean she didn't wrestle with God on many occasions. She let him know when she was angry, frustrated, and hurting. She also celebrated with him when she was happy, excited and full of joy. She leaned on him for strength and trusted in him for everything. Her faith simply did not waiver. Christ was her solid rock.

She always had a way of making everyone believe that they were her favorite. Yet, even after all she taught me, especially the way she was kind to the unkind, the way she cared for the uncaring, and the way she loved the unlovely, I would be kidding myself, if I believe anything other than Grandpa was the love of her life -- and Jesus was her favorite.

My grandma taught me to always love Jesus. Because he was her favorite, everyone else she met felt like they were her favorite as well. There is nothing more important in life than relationships. If your most important relationship is Jesus, then all others will fall into place.

STEFF WOELL is a mother of four daughters in the northwest suburbs of Chicago. She is doing her best to love Jesus and serve Him each day. She is grateful for her amazing husband and the support he gives her to be her broken self and explore life together. She has been abundantly blessed with a large extended family, a great church home, friends she admires and loves, and her own heaven on earth in Arcadia, Michigan.

RUTH SCHWENK

I Want My Daughter to be a Mom

A few years ago, my husband and I attended our daughter's kindergarten graduation. There was quite a bit of fanfare surrounding this event. There was food, beverages, and an inspiring story-time for the students. The parents were outfitted with grins and video cameras.

Before the conclusion of the ceremony, each student was asked to walk up to the podium and share with the audience what they wanted to be when they grew up. One by one, each student announced their desired profession. The list went a little something like this:

"I want to be a teacher."
"I want to be the next American Idol."
"I want to be a fire fighter."
"I will play football."
"I am going to be a doctor."

The students smiled with a hint of accomplishment, paused for the applause, and then posed for their parents' Kodak moment. Each goal was a good one, and in many ways, predictable. What was surprising, though, was what wasn't on the list. Later in the day as we were thinking about the ceremony, it occurred to us that there wasn't one girl in the class who said, *"I want to be a mom when I grow up."*

11

I couldn't help but wonder if being a mom was becoming less desirable or noble than other pursuits. I want my daughter to see the calling of motherhood as significant, world changing, and worth pursuing. I want my daughters to know that being a mom is something to which it's worth giving their lives.

The first description of how God sees children is found in Psalm 127:3. *"Children are a reward."* The Hebrew word for reward is *sakar*. It literally means a wage. It is a reward, wage, or payment that is given to someone. The psalmist is saying that children are like money paid out to someone who has empty pockets. This is what the Bible is saying about the gift of parenting. It is a payment that should be received joyfully, but also handled wisely.

The Creation account explains that children are image bearers of God as well. Genesis 1:27 (NIV) says,

> *27 So God created man in his own image,*
> *in the image of God he created him;*
> *male and female he created them.*

Adam and Eve were given an *identity* and a *mission*. Their primary identity was that they were created in the image and likeness of the Creator God Himself. The Hebrew word for image is *tselem*. It simply means that we bear the resemblance or similarities of God. As His creation, we in some way reflect who God is to the world.

The theme in the opening verses of Psalm 127 is basically that unless the Lord blesses our efforts to build, then our "labor is in vain." But what is interesting is that though the psalm starts out describing building a house and city, the author spends the entire second half describing children. Psalm 127:3-4 (NIV) says,

> *3 Sons are a heritage from the LORD,*
> *children a reward from him.*
> *4 Like arrows in the hands of a warrior*
> *are sons born in one's youth.*

Is there a connection between Solomon's theme of building and blessing a city with the building of our own homes and children?

I think being a mom is that important. I want to teach my daughter the lesson that being a mom isn't just okay, it is world changing.

. . . .

RUTH SCHWENK is the wife of a pastor, who is her best friend and the love of her life. She is a blessed homeschooling mother to her four beautiful children, and she eagerly awaits meeting her five others in heaven. Ruth is a graduate of Moody Bible Institute in Chicago. She has a passion for following God, leading worship, rescuing orphans, and inspiring others to create a God honoring family. She is the creator and editor of The Better Mom Website (www.thebettermom.com) where thousands of moms gather to share life, learn, and grow together.

SHARRON CARRNS

Passing On a Legacy of Prayer

My father died when I was a little girl, and my mother suffered from chronic illness that left her occasionally unable to care for my brother and me. In these times we would stay with my grandparents.

Grammy became a Christian while Grandpa was fighting in World War II. As a child her parents had taken her to "honky tonks," and to pass the time she learned to dance. One lonely day while Grandpa was away she heard music down the street. She followed the sound, thinking there might be dancing.

Instead, she stumbled upon a tent revival. Curious, she stayed to listen. At the end of that revival she went to the altar, got on her knees, and gave her heart to Jesus.

In the years Grandpa was away in the war, Grammy made a small country church her home. With the women of the church she learned what it meant to trust God completely, living out her faith at a time when she could have been paralyzed by fear or found some other way to try to ease her anxious waiting. Most of those women were waiting for their husbands, too.

There was no heat in their church, but they would gather anyway, staving off the bitter Wisconsin cold by wrapping blankets around their legs as they prayed with photographs of their husbands lined up in front of them.

One dark night, the women felt a strong nudging of the Holy Spirit to pray for my grandfather. They later learned that he had been on a mission so dangerous the men were required to pack their bags and write letters to their loved ones in case they did not return. Only my grandfather and one other man would ever come home.

When Grandpa did come home the war had ended. But the prayers of my grandmother did not.

The one lesson that became the most influential of all was the night my cousin was born. A frantic call from the hospital came in the middle of the night. The baby was in trouble. An emergency C-section was being performed. Grammy bolted into each of our rooms and pulled us right up out of bed with no explanation but, "Come on! We have to pray!"

Every one of us went to our knees in her living room praying. Today that young mother is a grandmother herself, and the cousin is a grown man with children of his own.

When I nearly lost two of my own babies, I remembered Grammy's example. And when one of my babies grew up and went to war in Iraq, I remembered Grammy's example. We went beyond asking others to remember us in prayer. We gathered our children and headed to the living room where we got on our knees and prayed. We pray together at meals, and at bedtime, and for any desire or concern of our hearts.

Our children are growing older now, and we are expecting our first grandchild. I've told them the stories of Grammy and her faith, and we have

SHARRON CARRNS has authored studies for fiction and non-fiction books, ministry and corporate training in her roles as Small Groups Director, Women's Ministries Coach, and Corporate Training Specialist. She has written leadership development and training programs for a division of a Fortune 500 company, corporations, government, non-profits, and the Army. Recent projects are the Working It Workbook for The Making of a Christian Best-seller by Ann Byle, discussion questions for Christy Award winning Hallie's Heart by Shelly Beach, and devotions as a contributing author for Faith Deployed… Again, by Jocelyn Green. She lives in Michigan with her husband and children.

followed her example. Because of Grammy, in good times and hard times we know to hit our knees.

If you or your family has not been open about praying it may feel awkward at first. But if you take the lead, over time it will become normal to pray in any circumstance. Don't talk about it first, don't merely ask your family members to pray about something. Instead, lovingly but boldly say to them, "Let's pray." Then begin. You will begin both a prayer and a legacy.

SHELLIE TOMLINSON

Adding Pearls

When I was a teenager, add-a-pearl necklaces were all the rage. They were a classic concept: a gift of a single pearl on a dainty chain given with the intention of adding other pearls on important holidays and special occasions.

Today, I think of add-a-pearls as a beautiful analogy of the accumulated wisdom we learn from our mothers. Oh, sure, we snicker as young girls. Not all of their advice strikes us as useful and some of it seems positively fossilized, but hopefully, over time and with the Father's blessing, we gain enough perspective to see that these mama-isms—the important values and the silly little lagniappe—are all unique treasures that only increase in value with the years in spite of any early resistance on our part.

My poor Mama exhausted herself trying to smooth the rough edges of her three little girls. Mama was a true "Southern lady," a natural beauty born the second of five to a Baptist preacher in Natchez, Mississippi. Her innate grace helped make her a basketball star; her black hair and bright wide smile topped a tall slender frame and earned her the hometown title of "Miss Forestry Queen."

Mama's marriage to her high school sweetheart ended shortly after she brought me, her third daughter, home from the hospital. Biological Dad was more interested in cards and liquor than diapers and bottles. Mama was raising three little girls on a clerk's salary when a childhood friend came to town and dropped by to pay her family a visit. It'd been years since that young man and Mama had seen one another. By this time he was fresh out of the service and farming a plot of land in Louisiana. For the next year or more he made the two-hour trip to court Mama. My sisters and I, ages two, three and five, were their ever-present chaperones. We rode in the back seat of his car and sang along with Mama to Conway Twitty's new hit song, *Mississippi Woman, Louisiana Man*.

It wasn't long before Papa married us, taking his prize bride and her tiny wedding party to the Delta to live on Bull Run Road. He built her a little white brick home with 900 square feet. She kept his castle spotless and worked beside him in the fields. In years to come, he would build her a larger house and she would tend it, too, with the same love and care than she gave the small one.

Mama looked as much a lady driving Papa's bean truck and grain cart during the day, as she did on the piano bench at Melbourne Baptist Church. Manners were important to Mama, a theme most of her lectures centered on, as she constantly schooled us in the things little ladies did and did not do. Unfortunately for Mama, my sisters and I had a hard time differentiating between the two. But, bless her heart, the woman persevered, leaving her precious pearls in every area of our lives.

Today, my sisters and I recognize the great legacy that is ours in the time-tested values our Southern Mama continues to pass on to her children, grandchildren, and now great grandchildren.

SHELLIE RUSHING TOMLINSON and her husband Phil live and farm in the Louisiana Delta. Shellie is the best-selling author of Suck Your Stomach In and Put Some Color On and Sue Ellen's Girl Ain't Fat, She Just Weighs Heavy. Tomlinson is owner and publisher of All Things Southern and the host of the weekly radio show All Things Southern heard across the South. When Shellie isn't writing, speaking, taping her show, answering email or writing content for the next deadline, you can find her playing tennis with Dixie Belle, (the chocolate lab who thinks she is in charge of running Shellie's life).

I'd love to think that everyone reading my words had a mother like mine, a woman of faith who taught me from childhood of the Risen Savior who saves souls and anchors lives. But, dear reader, if that's not your past, I hope you know it can be your future. I pray you'll be the one that begins such a legacy, and that you'll start building that heritage today. One pearl at a time.

Kit Kat

Easter, when the earthy smell of spring hangs in the air, colorful crocus and daffodils emerge from the snow, and church bells announce the resurrection of the Risen King. Every Easter, tall white lilies encased the communion table in my family's church. The sights and sounds of childhood Easter celebrations are memories I hold in my heart.

One particular Easter Sunday long ago, I wiggled free from my parents and maneuvered to sit between my grandparents. With my spiffy new white patent leather shoes and matching purse, I snuggled in the pew. During the service, I stealthily took chocolate eggs from my pocketbook, peeled the foil wrappers and popped the treats one by one into my mouth. My grandma would reach over, palm up, to collect the wrappers and quietly deposit them in her own purse. I was sure my mom never noticed. That was my grandma: friend, confidante, and partner in crime…even if it was only eating chocolate in church.

Her given name was Ruth Beatrice Elizabeth Smith. She preferred Kit Kat, maybe because she spoke with a lisp as a child. No one in my family remembers how the name came to be, but she was Kit Kat long before the candy bar was introduced. Born in 1908, God gave her 101 years on earth, to teach the rest of us how to live joyfully. "The Lord must have more work for me to do. Otherwise he would have taken me sooner," was her pat answer for why she lived to a ripe old age.

Each morning she would make her list, but not of things to do. Beginning with my mom, her only child, she would recite the full name, birth date and a special prayer for each family member. This was to keep her mind clear, or so she said. She fell asleep talking to God too.

Whenever I needed counsel in regard to friends or in later years, boys, Kit Kat was the one I'd often turn to for guidance. Her sage advice was always followed by, "I'll keep you in my prayers, Lovey."

My first Bible, illustrated with beautiful pictures, was from Kit Kat. Just what a child needed to become enamored with God's Word. When I got older, I was surprised to find out there was writing in her Bible. Underlined were verses that meant the world to her, especially the 23rd Psalm.

Walking through the valley of the shadow of death became very real as the two of us watched my grandpa's health decline. Comfort came from those words, peace and a promise. Kit Kat knew it was not the end. Her example of trusting in the words of God made quite an impression on a sixteen-year-old. And it was the beginning of note taking for me in my own Bible.

In my favorite photograph of Kit Kat and me, I am two years old. We are standing in front of the Lexington, an iconic supper club in St. Paul, Minnesota. My dad was behind the camera. My mother, grandfather, the senior pastor and his wife are also in the photo, with strikingly happy faces.

Kit Kat loved people completely. I think she was on to something. Her legacy of love lives on in her daughter, grandchildren and great grands. "The Lord has done great things for us, and we are filled with joy" (Psalm 126:3, NIV).

Kit Kat always saw the glass full, not half full, but overflowing. Her life was marked with prayer, the Bible and love. She made the world a brighter place as she shared her joy. That is my prayer, to be just like Kit Kat.

. . . .

BECKY DANIELSON, M.ED., is a licensed Parent & Family educator and coauthor of EMPOWERED PARENTS: Putting Faith First. She lives in Edina, MN with her husband, Scott, and two sons. The Lexington is still her favorite restaurant. www.beckydanielson.com

Life Lessons

My one and only child, John, called from college the other night. He was experiencing computer problems and by the sound of his voice he wanted me to fix it. And it sounded like the only fix was a new computer. That's what my mom ears were hearing, anyway.

When I hung up the phone my mind raced to where, when, how? How could I fix this for him? And how soon could I do it?

However, my husband asked, "Was John informing us of a problem or asking us to fix it for him?" At eighteen, he had to go beyond just presenting a problem to us. He needed to present possible solutions.

I was rushing to make everything better for him. After all, I'm his mom. But our job is to teach kids the life lessons that will keep them from being shackled by helicopter parents.

As Christian parents, our deepest desire is to see our child come to faith in Christ, but even beyond that, we desire to see them own their faith and walk closely with Christ. I think the biggest mistake I made was to think my son's walk with Christ would look like mine.

I loved attending youth group, reading the Bible, listening to Christian music. When John didn't seem to like any of these things, I confess, I panicked. I made him attend youth group. It was a fight every Wednesday night in middle school. His 8th grade year in the spring semester I picked him up at church after COW (Cloud of Witnesses). Instead of the usual frown, he had a smile on his face.

"What happened tonight?" I asked.

"Nothing."

"Something happened. I've never seen you this happy after COW," I said. John finally came forward with the reason for the smile. He said, "Tonight they asked people to get up and tell their story. It was so cool. There were couches up on the stage, and people went up and told their story. Mom, I went up and told mine."

"That's awesome, John. What did you say?" As usual, I was probably pushing too much. John informed me that what he said wasn't important, but that he liked COW now.

God heard the prayer of this mom's heart. Did I learn my lesson of not trying to squeeze John into my mold? What do you think? I had to learn how and when to push him, but not to push him into my mold. God had a John-shaped mold that looked very different from my mom shaped mold.

Here's what Romans 12:1 tells us, the J.B. Phillip's translation. "Don't let the world around you **squeeze** you into its own mold, but let God re-mold your minds from within, so that you may prove in practice that the plan of God for you is good, meets all his demands and moves towards the goal of true maturity."

The day my son told me "thank you" for making him go to youth group all those times, was the day I realized that God was working and creating John to be who God wanted him to be, not who Mom wanted him to be. And that computer, now that the decision making is on John's plate, well, we haven't heard a whole lot about it.

As I let go of my child and deposited him into the hands of God, I discovered that who God created our child to be, is exactly who we want him to be.

ANITA LUSTREA is executive producer and host of Moody Radio's Midday Connection. Garnering NRB's 2008 Program of the Year Award, Midday Connection is geared toward women who want to talk about the important issues of life. Anita is also a much sought-after conference and retreat speaker and lives in the Chicago suburbs with her husband, Mike, and son, John.

Unexpected Gift

*My purpose is that they may be encouraged in heart
and united in love, so that they may have the full
riches of complete understanding, in order that they
may know the mystery of God, namely Christ, in
whom are hidden all the treasures of wisdom and
knowledge.*

(Col. 2:2-3, NIV)

I stared at the neglected wooden box. It was a 1927 Lane Hope Chest—a symbol of hope and preservation. For months, I dared not open it. Cobwebs and dust blanketed the peeling veneer.

Grandma had died more than twenty-five years ago, leaving me with the neglected box and its secret stash of personal keepsakes.

Seeing Grandma in the eyes of my own girls, I longed to discover more about her life. She was never anything but old to me. Who was this woman who was addicted to Bingo, couldn't remember my birthday, and argued with me when we played Scrabble?

Mystery shrouded my grandmother, and this box held the answers. I wanted to lift the lid and discover order and beauty. I imagined finding a treasure chest of valuables, beautifully preserved for a future generation—for *me*. I fantasized about organized scrapbooks, cherished baby books and tiny trinket boxes filled with locks of hair or special notes.

Instead, the smell of mothballs and cedar assaulted me. Photographs, newspapers, and children's artwork all lay in a sticky, muddled heap. I struggled to make sense of the mess. *These aren't even labeled,* I thought. Squinting at a pair of blank eyes, I asked out loud, "Who are you?"

Silently, the photo echoed, "Who are *you?*" I couldn't imagine saving any of this stuff. I separated the photographs into a pile. (So old fashioned!) In another, I stacked the newspapers. (Wow! Astronauts Walk on the Moon!) I assembled the children's keepsakes. (Funny poems written by my dad and uncles!) I sifted through old menus, cards, and other souvenirs.

Then, a journal Grandma wrote while a student in nursing school. I fingered the frayed pages. She could not have known that decades later I would read her words. They were the words of a hopeful young girl on her way to becoming a woman, my grandmother before she was Grandma.

The careful cursive began: "I have reached the age of 20 years. Gee! But I feel like 16." Funny, coming from a woman who would be 104 if she were still alive today. She wrote in code and left blanks. Her secrets echo the ones I used to write about in my own journal. I, too, left blanks, embarrassed that someone might hijack my journal and discover my private thoughts.

As I began to piece together the story of Grandma's life, I discovered that she selflessly served her mentally handicapped daughter, raised four boys mostly by herself, and nurtured an absent, alcoholic husband. These relics depicted the disappointments and joys of her journey. Along the way, her choices revealed God's imprint on her life. She looked to him for solace and guidance.

It would have been easy to dismiss that old box as a worthless piece of junk. But by the time I finished sorting and salvaging all these mementos from the past, I realized the box contained a story, messy and complex, as life stories usually are.

I had to search for her, but the discovery was worth the effort. As the hope chest unites the generations, so God's love unites our hearts as we come to understand the mystery of his great love—Christ in us.

God transforms junk into jewels, and plants treasures of wisdom and knowledge in the hearts of those who seek him. Ultimately, my hope and future are in him alone.

I carefully arranged the souvenirs of a lifetime back in the chest. I will one day give this precious gift to my daughters, but my hope is that while I'm still living, they will see Christ in me.

CHANTEL ADAMS spent several years writing position papers for an association of state child welfare organizations. She is also the founder of The Princess Generation, a nonprofit organization whose mission is to redefine what it means to be a princess by raising up a generation of young women wholly devoted to putting others first. This is her first published essay.

My Angel Mother

All that I am or hope to be, I owe to my angel mother.

-- Abraham Lincoln

When I was growing up, my mom's passion was sewing. As I was her only daughter, and with four sons, Mom loved sewing girl clothes. The whir of her sewing machine often lulled me to sleep. When I woke up in the morning, a new outfit seemed to have magically appeared, hanging on my bedroom door. I was delighted.

One year, she sewed personalized felt Christmas stockings for each of us kids. We helped her decorate them with teddy bears, snowflakes, trains, and reindeer complete with red sequin noses. As a teenager, I followed her lead and sewed my first Christmas stocking as a gift for my boyfriend, Randy. I'm sure he was impressed with my handiwork—just what every 16-year old guy has on his wish list. But he must not have minded too much. Three years later, he married me!

Twenty years ago, my mom gave me a little stuffed angel she had created. The stuffed angel was much more than one of Mom's cute renderings, though cute was the only way to describe her. She had curly salt and pepper-colored yarn hair tied up on her head by a pink ribbon. She wore a pink chintz dress with a crocheted lace collar and matching wings. Her hands held a lacy heart with a tiny rosebud stitched in the center.

"This is for you," Mom said, proudly holding the angel out to me. "You can think of me watching over you. She does look a little like me, don't you think?"

I nodded, trying not to let any tears escape—at least not any Mom could see. I knew she had been worried about me—and rightly so. My marriage was in deep trouble and I had decided to separate from Randy. I placed the angel on my dresser where she reminded me of Mom's love.

That's when her weekly phone calls started. Like clockwork, Mom's cheery voice came on the line about the same time every week.

"Just wanted to check in to see how you're doing." She offered plenty of motherly advice and perspective from her wiser vantage point.

I'd sigh and listen and give thanks for having a mother who cared about me. I reported about my my first job since being a stay-at-home mom. I updated her on her grandsons' progress in school, and how Randy and I were trying to work things out.

Our conversations included my plans for a move to a small rural community where Randy and I would begin again. Mom continued to check in weekly, making sure I was settled and happy.

Years passed in a blink. All too soon, I found *I* was the one making the weekly phone calls to check on Mom. Dad had been diagnosed with dementia, and Mom was caring for him.

"Mom, I'm checking in to see how you're doing." I'd say in my cheeriest voice. Monday nights at 9:30 were our time to talk—after she had completed Dad's nightly routine.

Recently, during our weekly phone call, Mom confided that she'd had a breast biopsy. Her doctor had called that day with results. "It's cancer," Mom said matter-of-factly.

I tried to take in what she was saying. Later that night, I picked up the little stuffed angel who still sat on my dresser. I remembered how Mom had so faithfully watched over me all those years, how her sweet creation had been a symbol of her love.

Several weeks later, I had the privilege of being with Mom for her surgery. I kissed her forehead as the nurse wheeled her into the operating room. I thanked the Lord for this beautiful angel Mom. And I prayed that I could also be an angel for her.

Lord, please help me take every opportunity to give back a small portion of all I've received from my mother.

DEB KALMBACH is the coauthor of Because I Said Forever: Embracing Hope in a Not-So-Perfect Marriage and the author of a book for children, Corey's Dad Drinks Too Much. She has also contributed to The New Women's Devotional Bible and Pearl Girls: Encountering Grit, Experiencing Grace. She speaks to women about the real hope we have in Christ for facing real life issues. Deb and her husband, Randy, have recently celebrated 40+ years of not-so-perfect marriage. They live in a tiny town in eastern Washington State. www.debkalmbach.com

Following In Her Footsteps

When my mother died, my sister turned to me with tears in her eyes and said, "She has such big shoes to fill. How can we possibly fill them?"

"The other problem," I quipped, "is that there are so many of them!" My mother, Ruby, had well over a hundred pairs of shoes—maybe two hundred. The zebra-skin heels with matching purse were my favorite. I also remember her joy at acquiring the beach sandals with Swarovski crystals on them. Her dogs were never dull.

My brother reminded us how, at age ten, my mother had only one pair of shoes and was embarrassed because they were actually boy's shoes. Even worse, she had to put cardboard inside to cover the holes in the soles. As an adult, Mom indulged in her inner child's constant craving for shoes that were feminine and stylish.

Ruby's legend loomed large because of how far her feet had carried her in those shoes. She remembered walking a mile past the beautiful, well-equipped "white" school to attend the run-down, segregated school for blacks. She prayed as she walked that someday she would have a chance to make a difference in a school like the one she attended. Leaving behind a childhood of poverty—with an alcoholic mother, a father who left before she was born, and the violent racism of the south in the 1940s—my mother rose to earn a Ph.D. in education, write her dissertation on desegregation, and fulfilled her prayers as the principal of an inner-city school in California. She was on a mission from God.

Ruby instituted a program for learning foreign languages, sent students to compete in Shakespeare competitions, and re-branded the school as "Lincoln Prep School" instead of Lincoln High School. She cared about all the students there—even the ones who would never go to college. I remember her telling me how proud she was that she convinced one of the troublemakers—a gang member and drug dealer—to earn his high school diploma. He loved her so much that he kept much of the drug trade off her campus out of respect. She couldn't fix everything, but she wanted each person to be a little better, whatever that meant. Like Jesus, she loved every single child... no matter what.

As my brother, my sister, and I planned her funeral service, we began to see that the mortuary parlor would not even begin to hold all her mourners. We booked the outdoor amphitheatre in Balboa Park. Even that huge venue was standing room only.

Mom always dreamed that the gospel choir from Lincoln Prep would sing at her final celebration. However, the school had closed down and the choir was long disbanded. But, miraculously, upon learning of Ruby's passing, a phone chain was instituted to re-unite the singing group. On the day of her funeral the Lincoln Gospel Choir reunited, in their old uniform gowns, to sing their beloved "Dr. C" back home. When we looked up on that stage, we knew that nothing is impossible with God.

No one person could possibly fill her shoes; not all of them. But as I stood in the amphitheater that day, I asked everyone there to metaphorically take one pair of Mom's shoes and wear them into the world. I asked everyone there to think of a characteristic about her they loved and try to be a bit more like that from now on; as if by donning her footwear each of us could be more kind to strangers, more willing to help a child, more funny, more eccentric, more able to heal past hurts. If each of us took up only one pair of those outrageous shoes and brought a little more Ruby into the world, it would be a better place.

. . . .

Despite being an amputee since age five, **BONNIE ST. JOHN** has sought to live up to her mother's legacy by winning Paralympic medals in ski-racing, graduating from Harvard, earning a Rhodes Scholarship, and being awarded an honorary doctorate for a lifetime of inspiring others with her books, training programs, and public appearances. With her daughter, Darcy, she has written her latest book on women leaders called, "How Great Women Lead: A Mother-Daughter Adventure into the Lives of Women Shaping the World." For more information, please visit www.bonniestjohn.com.

"It is up to us," I told those gathered, "now that she found out how to use her Ruby slippers and go home at last."

Coming of Age

Women have a communal understanding of the ups and downs of femininity. Even if we've not yet met, I *get* you. You *get* me. We speak a common language. Who could forget the uninvited force of nature that whips us into womanhood?

It was a very typical day in my thirteenth year. My brother, five years older, was tormenting me. This was certainly nothing new. More than twice my size, he could swat me like a fly and had been inventing new terms of endearment for me since birth.

With my budding individuality came a keen sense that this was unfair. I promptly reported my offender with the hope of gaining a bit of maternal sympathy, or at least a reprieve from my brother's bullying. Much to my dismay, my mother's advice was this: "If you would just ignore him, he would stop doing it. He only does it to hear you holler!"

Though this was a typical response from my mother, my heart awakened to deep pain. My new perception was enraged injustice. I felt like no one even cared! I curled up on the floor in a corner of the living room. In my teenage turmoil, I prayed, "Someday, when I am a mother, I want to remember being a thirteen-year-old daughter. Help me to understand where she is coming from."

Fast forward twenty-three years. Now *I* was the mother of a thirteen-year-old daughter. There was no bullying brother in this family picture. Yet, the pattern of my childhood pursued me into marriage. I was battered by a man seven years my senior.

I began a vigil of marching the perimeter of land surrounding our home: crying, searching, seeking answers. I would walk until my legs could no longer carry me. My thirteen-year-old heart was resurrected within my thirty-six-year-old carcass with that same tidal wave of desperation.

With no one to plead on my behalf, I again presented my case before God. The prayer I had prayed at thirteen and the prayer I launched on my private march were both answered in one mother-daughter conversation.

Nicole was thirteen, just turning fourteen when she shared her tortured heart. As her story unraveled, my worst fears were acknowledged. My husband had been sexually abusing her.

"Why didn't I see this offense?" Yet the pieces fit like a sinister puzzle. I didn't think twice. Knowing my daughter was right, we fled. I sought legal advice and reported the abuse to Children's Services. We left home and found shelter with my mother.

Who would have ever imagined that the desperate prayer for justice breathed by a thirteen-year-old girl, barely coming of age, would have such a profound effect on the future?

As we bandaged our wounds and picked up the pieces, we were bound in secrecy, pain, and shame. But, as we began to heal, we both realized that being silent would only allow the travesty of sexual abuse to continue. So, we told and told and told again...and again...and again. The more we share what happened to us, the more we discover we are not alone.

Unfortunately, with one in six girls reportedly being sexually abused by the age of eighteen, we are among many.

Mothers, it is ever so urgent that we not forget what it's like to be a daughter; to be ever available to hear and protect her innocent heart. It is also never too late to do the right thing: to say "I'm sorry" and come to the aid of your child.

Daughters, no matter what your age, it is vital to identify and acknowledge infractions and injustices. Don't be afraid or ashamed to *tell* and tell again until you find that special sister, mother, grandmother, or daughter who will hear your cry for freedom and help deliver you.

CYNTHIA (CINDY) STIVERSON is a speaker, writer, and artist. In 1998, God inspired her to launch Woven: Women of Virtue Network, a spiritual formation and friendship ministry for women. She pastors women at Newark Church of the Nazarene in Ohio. Cindy considers raising her daughter, speaker/author Nicole Braddock Bromley, to be her greatest contribution to the world. She loves the men in her life: husband Mark, son-in-law Matt, and treasures her role as "Grammy" to Jude and Isaac.
www.WovenWomen.blogspot.com
www.CynthiaStiverson.com

ELISSA M. SCHAUER

●

Take Heart

Remember: life is hard, but God is good.

I've read it other places since, and even heard it in a song, but the first time I saw those words scrawled inside a card, I was only thirteen. School was *hard*. Friendships were *hard*. Life was *hard*.

My Mom *could* have dismissed my "struggles," since the overdramatized angst of a middle-class North American thirteen-year-old girl is all but insignificant. She could have tried promising that it gets easier after those turbulent adolescent years. Or she could have used that tired Christian-ese mantra that "God will not give us more than we can handle," a hopeful but fictitious theological stance.

But she didn't. She spoke the truth: life *is* hard. It's no secret, since our world is such a mess: disease, unemployment, murder, injustice… infidelity, addiction, narcissism, and on it goes. Real problems, with no end in sight. As an adult, I waver between fury and heartbreak when I contemplate all that is wrong in this life.

As a parent, it's tempting to deny the reality of pain and instead opt for a shiny, happy take on life. There is no part of me that wants to tell my children of the world that awaits them. I want to shield them from awful things and create our own safe little kingdom. The danger is that, of course, reality eventually seeps through the cracks of our well-constructed fortress. And then what? When bad stuff happens—not *if*, but *when*— how will my children respond?

36

We cannot avoid pain in a world stained by depravity. Jesus said it this way: *In this world you will have trouble.* Not "may" or "might," but *will.* It *will* be hard, and there *will* be pain because there *will* be trouble.

My mom's statement was not an admonition to wallow in the sadness of it, nor to brace myself for the fight, but to acknowledge it. To call a spade a spade. No matter how much we wish things were different, trouble is unavoidable.

If we could absorb the important lessons of life yet avoid the painful learning curve, we'd all sign up. So my mom acknowledged the fickle nature of teenage friendships while encouraging me to do the hard work required of relationships, knowing all the time that adult relationships require even *more* effort.

The Bible is filled with stories of men and women who experienced the difficulties of life, all given much *more* than they could handle: Abraham, Moses, Joseph, Elijah, Mary, and the Disciples, just to name a few. Nowhere does God make a deal with his followers to make things easy.

Thankfully, there is a second part to the lesson. There is a "but" that changes everything: Life is hard, *but* God is good. Take heart! You may feel as if the waves will overcome you, sucking you into the undercurrent of trouble. But God is good, and he has overcome the troubles of this world. There is Hope, and his name is Jesus.

God promises to go with us, to never abandon us, to see things through, and that *all* of it—even the bad stuff—can be used for His good and His glory. It's through the challenges of life that we learn to depend upon him and even become desperate for Him. Oftentimes, the goodness of God is most evident in the trials of this life, a lesson I first heard as a teen from my Mom, but am continuing to learn each day.

ELISSA SCHAUER is a writer living near Chicago, IL with her husband and three children.

Remember: life is hard, but God is good.

Becoming a Mother

How I Had a Baby, Lost a Husband
and Found God's Grace
in the Delivery Room

The ending of my story is much better than the beginning, which starts when I left my husband while nine months pregnant. "Left" is a euphemism for two girlfriends coming over to my house in San Francisco and helping me pack as much stuff as possible while my then-husband sat in the corner, vacillating between incredulous indignation that I would have the audacity to read his private emails on his "secret Blackberry," and complete panic that his wife and baby were walking out the door.

Meanwhile, the day was hot, the baby was kicking and I had no patience for his mood swings, especially after he told me only a few weeks earlier that he wasn't sure he could do the whole baby birth thing. "Maybe you should find a new coach," was exactly what he had said, which I soon learned was code for "I'm having an affair."

So there I was two weeks later, in labor at my sister Stephanie's house in the suburbs of Chicago. The pain started around 1:30 AM. By the time my sister Casey and sister-in-law Jen arrived, it was pretty intense. By then, the sun was on the verge of rising and Steph had already finished packing my hospital bags and making sure the car seat was ready. I was lying on the couch eating a Krispy Kreme doughnut while Jen and Casey read aloud stories from magazines. I tried to listen but my mind was racing. My life was such a mess How was I ever going to become a mother?

It was just about noon when my soon-to-be-ex arrived from San Francisco. He looked tanned and well rested, but his color soon drained when the gravity of what was happening dawned over him. "I can't believe it," he whispered, staring at my belly. "We're having a baby."

Casey, Stephanie and Jen shot him the Vulcan death stare. "Hey, Captain Obvious," Stephanie said, handing him a notepad and stopwatch. "Start timing the contractions." Of course Stephanie was timing them as well, but I think she wanted to give him something to do.

When it was time to go to the hospital, he insisted on driving me. "I need some time to talk to my wife," he said (because nothing says "good time to talk" like a drive to the hospital when contractions are 10 minutes apart). Stephanie hesitated, but eventually acquiesced, adding, "We'll follow in my car, so don't take any shortcuts." Game on!

By the time we got to the hospital it was 4 PM and I was begging for an epidural and a muzzle. The muzzle was for he who was driving me crazy. Why couldn't we talk about something normal like names or nursery colors? He just kept going on and on about sorry he was for what he had done. According to him, it was nothing more than an innocent flirtation that spun out of control, and he was "pretty sure" he loved me and not the other woman. (And I was pretty sure I wanted to clobber him!)

Despite my anger and heartbreak, I asked him to be my coach in the delivery room. It wasn't that I wanted to save our marriage. I was "pretty sure" our marriage was over, but I knew having a baby—having our baby—was not about me, or my husband. Having a baby is a gift from God. There was nothing that would stand in the way of me giving our son everything he needed and deserved, which included having his father present when he took his first breath.

It was at that moment that I knew I had become a mother.

BETH ENGELMAN is single mom living large on a shoestring budget. Her website, www.mommyonashoestring.com, is all about crafts and activities families can do without breaking the bank. Her column "Mommy on a Shoestring," appears in over 30 local papers around the Chicago area as well as on the Chicago Sun-Times / Pioneer Press website where you can also view her "MOAS" video series. Beth is an "ivoice" contributor to NBC Universal iVillage where she reports on stories that affect her community. She holds a master's degree in Education and has written several interactive children books and games.

LORI KASBEER

Strength In The Midst of Life's Storms

Now glory to God! By his mighty power at work within us, he is able to accomplish infinitely more than we might ask or think.

(Eph. 3:20, NLT)

The alarm clock sounds. I roll over to turn it off and begin another day. It is then I remember the baskets of laundry piled in the living room, the dining room table piled high with children's school work and leftover mail and dishes from last night's dinner filling the kitchen sink. Half-awake, struggling to find my feet for the day, I think back on the mothers who have come before me.

My grandmother raised five children on her own, while her husband was away earning a living as a railroad engineer. I wondered how she found the energy day after day. Her days began early and ran long as she single-handedly cared for a large family, while working at her own job as an elementary school teacher. Yet while growing up around my grandmother, I never remember hearing her complain. Instead I remember watching her incorporate exercise moves while cleaning the house. "Come on, Lori, get in shape while cleaning!"

Then I think of my aunt who, late in life, faced raising her two grandchildren when her own daughter developed a debilitating

41

disease. Serving as a parent again in the twilight years proved challenging, especially since she was simultaneously struggling to find the best possible medical care for her own daughter. With the loving support of her husband, she tackled elementary and middle school, then high school with her granddaughters. Yet I often found her singing praises to the Lord.

I wonder how she did it. How did she get up day after day and with a song in her heart?

And then I think of my own mother. Mom worked hard raising three kids while working outside the home. Her health became a struggle, but she worked on and was getting ready to retire and relax. Then she discovered her kidneys were beginning to fail. Her retirement with her grandchildren and husband of forty-four years was in jeopardy.

Mom and Dad were faced with the possibility those years would be spent inside doctors' offices, that mom would spend hours hooked to dialysis machines. A kidney transplant was the only solution, but age guidelines limited how long she would be eligible for a transplant. Her disease had a genetic root, so she ruled out any of us children even being considered as donors, because it might jeopardize our own future health.

But from the beginning, God knew. He provided a husband who was a perfect match. They checked into the hospital together, where Dad gave Mom a healthy kidney and a new lease on life. She endured years of failing health and found the faith that God would provide, denying her own need in order to protect her children. How does a mother find this kind of inner strength?

Even burrowed under the pillow, I can hear rain drumming on the roof. A reminder that rains in life will come, and the strong current of life's disarray will tempt us to give in, but the one thing stronger is The Rock.

These women's strength in the midst of the life's storms is a legacy I can draw from. I roll out of bed to tackle the new day and its challenges, knowing His mighty power will give me the strength he gave my grandmother, my aunt, my mother.

It is through God's power in your life a younger generation of mothers can step into life's storms and accomplish more than ever imagined. You are a legacy of strength!

. . . .

LORI KASBEER, a lover of all things chocolate, has a house full of boys; three to be exact, however, if you add her husband, the cat, and the dog testosterone runs rapid. When she is not doing laundry and working full time for a large Florida school district, she is a Christian book reviewer for Lori's Book Reviews (www.lorisbookreviews.com). With a heart for women, she finds it a privilege to remind women today that God is deeply in love with them.

CARA PUTMAN

●

The Friendly Family: all part of our DNA

Some days you make a decision that impacts your family. Other days, you make a decision that impacts future generations. How well I remember one of those moments.

Starting in fifth grade, I was homeschooled. Imagine a time when homeschooling was new and more than a little odd. Because I was eleven, I was one of the older homeschoolers when we started. I'll never forget those awkward early days when everyone assumed the worst about why we homeschooled and how we learned to be polite and take the comments quietly. It was a lonely time that drew our family tightly together.

A couple years into our homeschool adventure, my mom set our family on a mission, one she hammered into our heads anytime we headed to an event or gathering. We would be the friendly family, the one that reached out to new families when they came to various get-togethers and meetings.

Sometimes as kids we rolled our eyes. Sometimes we shrugged and went along. But at a certain point, this call to friendliness entered the DNA of our family…at least in my mind.

One crisp fall day we were driving the back roads to a farm tucked among the rolling hills of Western Nebraska for a hayrack ride. I couldn't wait for the bonfire and time with friends when Mom issued her routine instruction to make sure we spent time with and befriended any new kids.

My brother groaned. "Why can't we hang out with our friends just this once?"

Mom looked over the headrest at him, that look in her eyes. You know the one. The gaze that brooks no argument because the answer doesn't even need to be said.

"We do it because we're the friendly family." I jumped into the fray. "It's who we are."

I'm sure my brother rolled his eyes, but he went along because that's what we did.

Now that I'm a parent, I'm always quizzing my mom for advice. How did she create the knowledge in each of us that we could be world changers? She's not sure. How did she reinforce something in our core that kept each of us from rebelling? Again, not so sure. But she mentioned this long ago event recently to illustrate how parents have the ability to choose the DNA of their families. Instead, of blindly repeating the past as we've seen it, we have the opportunity to choose a different course for our kids if we have the fortitude to do the work.

My daughter didn't appear engaged as we talked, but I've since learned just how closely she listened. Later she asked if that was why I made her sit next to the new girl when one arrived at her gymnastics team. Or when I strongly encouraged the kids to invite other kids over to help introduce them to each other. After listening to the conversation Mom and I had, she came up to me.

"Is that why I have to be friendly?"

"What?" I wasn't sure what she meant.

"You know. Why we always have to sit next to the new kid and be nice."

I smiled. "Yes, it is."

CARA C. PUTMAN lives in Indiana with her husband and four children. She's an attorney, teacher at her church, and contract lecturer or adjunct faculty at a local community college and a Big Ten University. She has loved reading and writing from a young age and now realizes it was all training for writing books. An honors graduate of the University of Nebraska and George Mason University School of Law, Cara loves bringing history and romance to life. Learn more about Cara and her books at www.caraputman.com.

45

"I guess we're the friendly family, too."

That's when I knew she got it. Now, that need to reach out to others and befriend the new or lonely has become part of our family DNA, too.

Grandma's Golden Bowl

A crowd gathered around me to thank me for speaking at the morning's brunch. It was the first time I've ever spoken for a group where most of them could somehow put together that they were related to me, regardless of how distant the connection was. One lady at the back patiently waited until she had my full attention.

"Your grandmother and I were friends." She reached out her aged hand to grasp mine. Her grip was tight. "When she married that Neufeld I wondered what would become of her. And all of us –" she swooped her hand as if toward an imaginary crowd "– said to each other, 'Can anything good ever come out of that family?'"

A small, frail step brought her close enough so I could see the glistening in her eyes. Her cheeks, crinkled with lines brought on by years of life, now doubled their wrinkled beauty as she smiled. "But look at you. I shouldn't be amazed at what God has done, but I'll say it anyway. It's amazing! In your family there are so many preachers, teachers, and wonderful people like you living for God and telling the world about it. God bless you."

With her words, I was transported back to my breakfast table decades ago.

"So Grandma, did you have a good sleep?" She was so old. How does a teenager start a conversation with an ancient woman?

47

"As good as usual." Never a woman of many words, she rarely gave more answer than what she was directly asked. It made talking with her a real chore for me.

"Don't you usually sleep well?"

She took a sip of her warm water, then carefully set the cup on the table. "I usually only sleep for two to three hours, and when I sleep, I sleep well."

I was trying to fit this with the pattern I'd seen. Every night she said good-night early, closer to eight o'clock than nine, going to her room and not coming out until morning.

"So Grandma, then why do you go to bed so early?" I wanted to be respectful, but it made no sense at all.

"Because if I didn't go to bed that early I wouldn't have enough time."

Now I knew she was off her rocker. "Time for what?"

"For praying. I have children, and grandchildren, and great-grandchildren, and there are more great-grandchildren and great-great-grandchildren still to be born. I need to pray for them. I'm getting old and I don't know how many nights I have left. Some nights I pray that God won't let me sleep so I can have more time to pray."

I struggled with even five minutes of dedicated, on-track, true praying time. How could my grandma spend hours doing what seemed so hard to me?

"Grandma, do you pray for my children?"

"Yes, and their children too."

Now, at the ladies' brunch, I was overwhelmed with thankfulness for this grey-haired beauty whose words awakened my heart to the gift Grandma gave me so many years ago.

I no longer wonder where I got the idea, about ten years ago, to spend every wakeful night-time moment in conversation with Jesus. When my children come to me and say, "Mama, I can't sleep," it's been my practice to ask them if they've talked to Jesus, sending them back to use any sleepless seconds in prayer.

Revelation 5:8b (NLT) says, *"Each one had a harp, and they held gold bowls filled with incense, which are the prayers of God's people."* In heaven there are beautiful bowls holding Grandma's prayers until the right time comes for them to be answered. Now, decades later, my Grandmother's prayers are being poured out.

CARLA ANNE COROY is a Christian speaker and blogger, and the author of Married Mom, Solo Parent. She ministers to a wide audience through her website and blog at carlaanne.com. Carla Anne has served full-time with organizations such as Youth for Christ and Crown Financial Ministries, and is currently developing an international mentoring organization for youth and a ministry to wives who parent alone. She also serves as a staff writer for the online magazine Mentoring Moments for Christian Women. Carla Anne lives in Canada with her husband and four homeschooled children.

A Mom Who Keeps Her Promises

My five-year-old son Dylan sat cross-legged on the ground, playing at the foot of my desk while I worked on the computer. Since he'd been out-thinking me from the time he was two, I shouldn't have been surprised at the conversation that ensued.

"Mom," he started simply, never taking his eyes off his toys. "When you were little, did Grandma ever tell you she'd get you a pony and then didn't?"

"No, she didn't," I answered. I stopped typing, swiveled my chair and rested my elbows on my knees and chin in my hands, wondering where this line of thought would go.

"Well, you told us you'd take us to Toys R Us this summer and you didn't. That's a true lie," Dylan proclaimed, his toys forgotten in his indignant challenge.

I sat back in my chair, crossed my arms and stared, speechless.

I was shocked that he remembered a promise from three months back, and stunned by his reasoning. But in the midst of being impressed by how his mind worked, I was convicted. He was right! Every time we drove past the toy store, my three little boys asked to stop and I'd put them off. Taking three boys into a toy store was pure torture.

My work could wait. Joining Dylan on the floor, I sincerely apologized for not following through on my commitment.

It's tempting to think my kids will understand when my schedule changes and it becomes inconvenient to keep a commitment. After all, they are "just" kids. Right? Wrong! I've discovered that after God and my husband, my children are the most important people to whom I should honor a promise.

The truth is while children may *say* they understand when we don't keep a promise, depending on their ages, it's really hard for them to fully grasp our complicated lives. All they know is they are eating a cafeteria lunch alone when mom said she'd bring a Happy Meal. Or they are in front of a TV when mom promised to take them to the park.

We need to teach children to be flexible, but a mom who consistently backs out of promises will teach her children to do the same. To become mothers who keep their promises, we need to guard our words and follow some daily practices.

Probably the biggest lesson I learned was never to say "yes" to stop nagging. The child learns he can eventually wear mom down, so the nagging increases. I learned to say "Let me think about it." Then I had to actually do that and provide a thoughtful answer.

Scheduling your promises can help you honor them. If you've promised to go to the zoo or work on a jigsaw puzzle together, put it on your schedule. That way it doesn't fall off your radar screen, and your child will feel honored.

Sometimes I feel overwhelmed by my child's requests. I've discovered there is usually a deeper motivation, a deeper need, than going to the mall or buying a new toy. If the request has more to do with spending time together than going to the park, I offer an alternative rather than commit to something I probably can't do.

A mother has the high calling of modeling the faithfulness of God to her children. In our busy

GLYNNIS WHITWER is on staff with Proverbs 31 Ministries as the Senior Editor of the *P31 Woman* magazine. She is one of the writers of *Encouragement for Today,* the Proverbs 31 e-mail devotions, with over 500,000 daily readers. Her newest book, *I Used to be So Organized,* has just been released. Glynnis, her husband Tod, and their five children live in Glendale, Arizona. Visit www.GlynnisWhitwer.com or www.HerOrganizedLife.com to learn more.

lives, it's easy to let promises to our children slip to the bottom of our to-do lists. Over time, this habit will weaken the trust our children have in us. More than listen to our words, children watch our actions. Will they find a mother who keeps her promises? If so, it will lead them to a God who keeps His promises.

Celebrating the "Special"

Above my little girl's closet door hangs an unassuming metal sign that simply says, "Celebrate." It doesn't quite match the décor, but there it stays. It reminds me of my mother because it embodies a legacy she continues to live out—the legacy of making time for special things that delight the heart.

My mother instilled in me the value of our heart's dreams. Ever since my inkling for story-telling turned into a "book" during fourth-grade Young Author days, my mom has never ceased to cheer on that passion. When I was a twentysomething, preoccupied with too many jobs and chasing a social life, she'd often take my writing dream down from the shelf and dust it off, with a reminder that she believed I had something to say.

But it's not just career goals. My mom understands how to bolster the spirit. Through her example, I've learned that being present at endless games, recitals, and school events sends the life-shaping message to a child: someone's always on their side. When I feel the crush of a deadline and my patience wears thin from my small children's needs, I recall how my mother has always been willing to put aside her to-do list for a cup of tea or a heartfelt chat that gives the soul a lift. And you know what else? My mother gets that a new pair of earrings does make a girl feel special. Frivolity in its place is worth gold. Mom understands balancing work and play.

And nobody does Christmas like my mother (except, perhaps, my father). I'm not merely talking of presents wrapped under the tree. Above all, Christmas has always meant rejoicing in our Savior's birth, and that includes creating a celebration atmosphere unique to the month-long season.

My mom would send us off to school with a traditional Norwegian Kringla warm from the oven. At day's end we'd stomp the snow from our boots just before she set warm mugs of cocoa on the table, while Bing or Perry, Nat or Andy crooned carols in the background. Homemade stockings, a bedecked tree, holiday programs at school and church, a nativity scene hand-painted by her own mother, sharing every Christmas with a lonely, somewhat cantankerous elderly woman who had no family of her own . . . my mom knows how to warm the heart.

I miss her. When I got married and moved south nearly a decade ago, I underestimated the losses I'd feel not being able to drop by my parents' home, not being able to meet her at the mall for spur-of-the-moment shopping fixes, not watching old movies with hot drinks in hand any old time we chose. I don't want to make her cry, mind you. But then again, if she sheds a few tears reading this, then we can share a mother-daughter moment across the miles, because my eyes keep blinking back emotion as I type. So . . .

Thank you, Mom, for celebrating me for the past four decades. Today, I celebrate you. Thank you for the legacy of giggling with me through the funny times, smiling through the teary ones, and always

ERIN KEELEY MARSHALL is the author of Navigating Route 20-Something (Harvest House, 2008) and The Daily God® Book (Tyndale House, 2009). In addition to her essay in Mother of Pearl, she is a contributing writer for Mornings with Jesus 2012 and Mornings with Jesus 2013 (Guidepost Books), due to be released next year. She edits and writes from home while growing as a mom to her two children, Paxton and Calianne, and as a wife to her husband, Steve. In her spare time she enjoys exercising, outdoor activities, decorating, cooking/baking, traveling, and hanging out with her family.

being there to bolster my heart. Thank you most of all for sharing the Savior of our souls with me.

You are the mother and grandmother so many children only dream of having. I pray that my own precious little ones and all their cousins will be enriched by your legacy. You bring so much "special" to our family. I'm cheering you on, and I love you!

Celebrate someone today. They will be blessed by you—and you'll be blessed in return.

Cool Grandma

"I am going to be the coolest Grandma ever!" I declared when my sweet daughter and son-in-law announced they were expecting.

My husband, to say the least, was in denial. He wasn't ready for the title of "Grandpa." He associated the name with gray-haired, walk-with-a-cane gentlemen. To him, who works out regularly in a gym and can out-bench-press men half his age, he just wasn't sure he fit the grandfatherly mold.

However, I never pictured myself as a cookie-baking, apron-wearing little lady with pinch-nez glasses and hair tied up in a gray bun. Nope, not me! I was going to be the "cool" Grandma!

I wasn't going to go as far as to ride a Harley motorcycle or anything, but I thought about all the things I would do with my grandbaby…fishing, camping, hiking, biking, swimming, bug-hunting, mud-pie making, tree climbing, and playing video games! Granted I'd have to learn how to somehow forego my fear of heights to climb trees, but I'd push past the fear.

I would spoil my grandchild with lavish, noisy gifts. The louder the better! "You say you want a jet propelled tricycle with an air horn, Grandbaby? Sure! Grandma will get it for you!" No request denied. "You want me to come sky-diving with you, Grandchild? I'll book an appointment with a hypnotist first to get over my fear of heights… and of falling…then we'll go!"

"You're the coolest Grandma ever!" I'd hear him say and I'd smile while putting icepacks on my tender, aching muscles.

My husband laughed at me when I told him all the things I'd do with my Grandbaby. "You don't do half that stuff now!"

When he's right, he's right. I had to admit that my living up to the "Cool Grandma" title was going to be hard.

On Feb. 20, 2011, my grandson was born. As I held him in my arms for the first time I fell instantly in love. I recalled holding my own three babies for the first time, knowing that each of them were God's gifts to me, but now, holding this new life, I praised God anew. As I gazed at his tiny face, I breathed out a whisper and a prayer, "Lord, help me become the 'Coolest Grandma' ever!"

My daughter, watching us from her hospital bed, raised her eyebrows in question. "Coolest Grandma? What do you mean by that? Are you getting a Harley?"

I laughed and shook my head. I realized then that "cool" has nothing to do with daring to do extreme activities with my grandson so he will approve of me. It also has nothing to do with spending money on extravagant noisy toys that he will discard after a little while.

No, "cool" must be defined by God's standards, not the world's. Only with God's help can I become a "Cool Grandma."

With God's help:

— My arms will always be available to give him a hug when he needs one.
— My face will always try to show him a smile, even when he doesn't deserve one.
— My voice will always try to express to him words of encouragement, words of comfort, and words of hope so he knows he can always talk to Grandma about anything.
— My thoughts will always be with him, even when he's far away, and he'll always know that he is prayed for daily.

— My life will always try to model what it means to love the Lord with all my heart, mind and strength, so my grandchildren will never wonder Whom their Grandmother serves.

...and *maybe* someday I might let him take me for a ride on *his* Harley!

LYNN DOVE calls herself a Christ-follower, a wife, a mom, a grandmother, a teacher and a writer (in that order). Lynn is the author of the Christian contemporary " Wounded Trilogy " for teens and young adults. Her books are listed as resources on the largest anti-bullying website in the world: www.bullying.org. Lynn's blog, " Journey Thoughts " was the 2011 Winner of a Canadian Christian Writing Award. Lynn lives with her husband and family just north of Cochrane, Alberta, Canada.

●

Precious Time

She was lying on the floor coloring. The ringlets from her baby soft hair cascaded over her shoulders and formed a perfect curl on the color filled page. At two years of age, her ability to stay focused on a task provided a sense of wonder to me and a tinge of envy from my mom friends.

I was tempted to continue to busy myself and mark off yet another item from the never ending "to do list." Instead, I nestled down beside my sweet daughter, grabbed a crayon and proceeded to join in on the uncomplicated, joyful simplicity of creating bursts of Crayola gladness on an otherwise stark grey and black lined coloring book page.

I am not sure how many crayons we have pared down to a nub over the years, but each one brought with it more than a completed work of art…it afforded precious time together. More important than the vanishing wax sticks of color were the words spoken, the lying next to each other on the floor, gentle nudges, encouraging words and playful giggling.

God had cautioned me, through the words of my older sister, that spending time with and savoring every moment with my child should be my primary task of daily mom life. I could allow the dust bunnies to multiply, as their time for my attention would come far sooner than I might like.

My heart is full to overflowing with a treasure trove of memories that surely would not exist were it not for the accepted wisdom given to me by my sister...and for that I am forever grateful. Little did she know that a simple suggestion would translate to my mom life being dedicated to intentional memory-making, and evolve into teenagers who make time for those they love.

A life observed is a life learned. My daily pursuit of reading God's word and praying for others was a modeled behavior that is now practiced by each of my teens as well. Each of my teens looks for opportunities to connect with the Lord and others. They choose God centered friendships and opportunities to serve. I have seen them set aside their agenda when a friend is in need. When their grandparents visit from out of state they make time for them. They take genuine delight in hanging out with us at home.

I frequently meet moms who lament that their teens are uninterested in togetherness, as their high school schedules are layered with hour after hour of personal pursuits.

Child see...child do.

Our children are watching, learning and absorbing how we do life. If we model busyness before relationship, that's what we will cultivate in our children. The choices we make in daily life become the legacy we leave behind.

In Matthew 22:37-38 when Jesus was asked what the greatest commandment was He instructed His followers to love God and love others. This sought-after love for God, and others, can only be attained by making time to grow in relationship. Much like the Pharisees who asked the question, we must all lay aside our own agenda and take time out of each day to put into practice Jesus' greatest commandments.

We must also be ever mindful that little eyes are watching...and learning.

Commit to spending time in God's word each day and model for your children the importance of your relationship with Christ.

Commit to investing in quality time with your children each day, even if it requires removing something from your daily schedule. Be assured that the investment of modeling relationship building to your children will provide dividends beyond your wildest dreams, for generations to come.

TRACEY EYSTER wife, mom, social media relationship gatherer and Creator/Editor of MomLife Today.com is a media savvy mom making a difference where moms are, on-line. Through speaking, writing and video interviews Tracey is passionate about encouraging, equipping and advising moms on every facet of momlife. She and her husband Bill live with their teens Samara and Westley on a ranchette in rural Arkansas. Visit her at her personal blog www.traceyster.com or connect with her on www.twitter.com/momblog

Keeping Jesus in the Family

A strange conversation occurred as my children and I sprawled across the cluttered living room rug. "Mom, do we have any more toothpicks? I need to finish this last little section of the road to Jerusalem."

"Uh oh, grab Jesus - He's about to fall off Battlecat! Can we get a real donkey next year?"

"Hey! You're supposed to throw the palmetto fronds in the road for Jesus, *not* poke your sister with them!"

"Mommy, can Skeletor be Pontius the Pilot? Where's his plane?"

It was Good Friday, and these bizarre comments were all part of our tradition of acting out the entire week preceding Easter, beginning with Jesus' Palm Sunday entry into Jerusalem and ending with His glorious resurrection. Our makeshift production, starring an actual Jesus doll I had purchased, was cast with a conglomeration of action figures, superheroes, Barbie, Ken and all their friends, GI Joes, and assorted plastic prehistoric beasties, whimsical creatures, and farm animals. All we needed were Buzz and Woody to look like a Toy Story Easter flick.

The mystery was that once each character was cast, it ceased to be an everyday toy. In our minds, the little doll was magically transformed a Bible character and we became completely enmeshed in the emotion and drama of the real Easter story.

Over the many years we performed our little play, the worst technical problem we encountered was when the pencils that were rubber-banded together to serve as a cross kept dumping the Ken-thief unceremoniously off the shoebox of Calvary. Oh, and let's not forget the time our dog chewed up GI-Judas and his thirty pieces of tin foil.

Ah, but those glitches were just small potatoes for us dedicated producers, intent on following the story line provided by our big picture Bible propped on the coffee table. Turning page by page, we recreated each scene of the Holy Week, culminating in the events of Good Friday, when the shoebox of Calvary doubled as a tomb containing the crucified body of Jesus carefully wrapped in a shroud of tissue paper. A large round pillow was rolled in front of the opening until Jesus sprang triumphantly from the grave on Easter morning.

I'll never forget the excitement of my little ones at daybreak each Easter as they raced to find the tissues discarded in a pile and Jesus miraculously sitting atop the shoebox tomb in his purple robe, his little plastic arms raised high in victory.

Unusual? Yes. A little corny? Probably. Memorable? Absolutely.

Our kids (and their parents!) loved this symbolic ritual honoring our Lord Jesus. It was a fun way to imprint these most important events, crucial to our faith, in their minds forever. And now that they're grown and having babies of their own, I've got my big picture Bible and all-star plastic cast ready and waiting for their curtain call.

Holiday traditions are as diverse as personalities. My friend Marianne wanted her children to respect the Jewish customs in which Jesus participated, so she established an annual family Passover Dinner (Seder) each Good Friday, pointing out the symbolism of various facets of Christianity as well as Judaism. This tradition now includes Marianne's grandchildren.

Faith-focused family traditions are important. They help children develop deep roots of security. Performing them together as a family elicits a sense of solidarity and cohesiveness through special memories they share with no one else.

. . . .

DEBORA M. COTY is a humorist, speaker, columnist, and award-winning author of over 100 articles and 13 inspirational books, including Too Blessed to be Stressed and More Beauty, Less Beast: Transforming Your Inner Ogre. Debora lives and loves in central Florida and is the mother of two grown children and wife of one who will never grow up. She's having a blast spoiling her first baby grand, Blaine. Visit with Deb online at www.DeboraCoty.com.

The psalmist knew this well when he said, "We will not hide these truths from our children but will tell the next generation about the glorious deeds of the Lord," (Psalm 78:4, NLT).

What better way to honor and enjoy truth than by starting a faith-focused family tradition this year?

Mother's Treasure

"And over all these virtues put on love, which binds
them all together in perfect unity."

(Col. 3:14, NIV)

Snow crunched under my boots as I gripped the cold metal handle of the glass door to the mall and tugged it open for Mom. Warm air rushed past, carrying the scent of cinnamon rolls and the cheery notes of *Jingle Bells* amidst the hustle and bustle of the holiday shoppers. After stepping inside, Mom and I reached for each other's hand. My weather-worn fingers slipped between her soft ones. Over a thousand miles had separated us the last thirty-plus years. Somehow the distance always melted away, without words, when we held each other's hand.

As we strolled through the mall, my hand, muscular from working outdoors with horses, engulfed her delicate silky one—but yet her hand, small as it was, had always been my strength.

Children giggled as they chased each other around the two-story Christmas tree, which towered over Santa's Workshop. Memories flooded back of the times when Mom held my hand as she led me to Santa, then gently lifted me onto his lap so I could tell him my dream—of owning my very own horse. Years later she made sure that dream came true.

Suddenly a little blond girl tripped and crashed to the floor. Her mother rushed over and held out her hand, lifting the sobbing girl. How often had Mom's hand pulled me up? So many times when I had fallen off my bike, she'd been there to wipe away the tears and pick the gravel out of my knees. When I got older, she boosted me out of my emotional wrecks. Her hand had cradled mine when I grasped a pencil and traced the alphabet for the first time. Years later she guided me through tough decisions. Life always became clearer and more focused when Mom held my hand.

I gave Mom's hand a squeeze. Over the past few years, the muscles in her hand had become smaller, her skin a bit thinner, and I cherished holding her hand more than ever before. When she held my hand she gave me courage and inspiration, almost as if she gave me a gift from God. A simple gesture—yet it was the reflection of her heart.

Time faded as we window-shopped our way down the hall. Brightly knit Norwegian wool sweaters hung on display at a gift shop. We paused and giggled as we reminisced of our trip to Norway. We were so engrossed in our conversation that when we turned to walk away, we unwittingly stepped directly in front of some people. We stopped. I was shocked to see that it was one of my friends with her teen daughter. Face to face we stood, me holding Mom's hand, and my friend holding her teen daughter's hand. The four of us smiled and glanced at each other knowingly—holding hands shares the greatest treasure of all, the love God placed in our hearts.

Fifteen years **REBECCA ONDOV** worked from the saddle in the Bob Marshall Wilderness, taking guests on horseback and packing their gear on mules over narrow and craggy trails of the Rocky Mountains. She says, "Everyday was an exciting adventure where I encountered everything from grizzly bears to forest fires." She's corralled these true-life stories in her devotional books and invites you to saddle up and ride with her, through the pages of her books, for an adventure of a life time. Rebecca founded Blazing Ink, inc., lives in Montana, and invites you to contact her through her website: http://RebeccaOndov.com

JULIA DAUGHERTY

Weight of Motherhood, Strength of God

Say the word *mother* and the images that come up seem limited. We have opened it up to include children who were not given life by you, who have been taken in and given their primary care by you, but other than that--that's it. We do not consider all of the ways we live as mothers in our communities.

I am a forty-year-old woman who lives with a family. There is a husband, a wife and three sons. I could tell the whole story of how I came to be this age with no children, even though I was married for seven years, but all you really need to know is that a desire of my heart was to have a house full of boys.

I no longer say that out loud after living here for two years. It's not because I had *no* idea what I was asking for, but mainly because God has redeemed and has given me my heart's desire.

I have a million and one funny and engaging stories I could share about the delicacy of being invited in to help parent children in the way I have. It takes more than I could ever muster. And thanks be to God for His love and gift of the Spirit, because otherwise the journey of learning to live as family might have killed all of us.

I came home one night, and everyone had already gone to bed except the oldest son. He often lurks in the kitchen trying to get my attention. He is sweet and kind and well, sixteen and all that implies. I am often irritated by his need for my attention, only because it mirrors my own insatiable need for communication. But as I have grown, I have come to love his desire to talk with me. I wish I had also matured in my ability to respond!

It was the night before the first day of school. He was sitting on the kitchen floor, and I asked him why. He said very quietly he didn't know. I asked him what was wrong and he said he was nervous.

I stupidly asked, "Why are you nervous?" I knew full well it was about school, but I couldn't get at what was making him nervous.

He said he didn't know, and right there I let him down. I said something short and curt about dealing with it and told him to just go get some sleep.

Before I got the fifteen steps to my room, I could see in my mind what could have been. How I could have sat with him on the floor and listened to his heart. How I could have been loving and compassionate and actually done something that would have helped him, at least for that night. It was the first time I actually felt the weight of motherhood. I felt regret and the real responsibility of having someone who is in need of selfless love from me. I went to bed with a heavy heart and a prayer of forgiveness for me and of comfort for him on my lips.

I felt in that moment the million opportunities that moms have every day to fail or succeed in loving their kids more than themselves. I hope to love him well next time. Only with God's strength I am sure!

"The love of correct grammar and a well-told story runs deep in Julia. This is no doubt partially due to the fact that her mother and grandmother are both English teachers. In college she fell in love with telling slice of life stories. These are moments from a day that, at the end of the day upon reflection, stand out with revelation or repentance, often both. You can find more from Julia on her blog, www.nohesitations.wordpress.com where writes on the most passionate topic of her life, living on mission through our identity found in the gospel of Jesus Christ.

Clean Heart, Dirty Diapers

As number twelve of thirteen kids, the last thing I worried about was infertility. I mean, come on—I was an aunt forty-five times, so obviously fertility wasn't an issue, right? My husband and I waited till our honeymoon, and the Bible says, "He honors those who honor Him," does it not?

And let's not forget I'm an inspirational author whose tagline is "Passion with a Purpose," so "passion" sure doesn't hurt either. All in all, a slam-dunk, right?

Well, a slam, anyway. Within a year there were progesterone/Clomid treatments, monthly ultrasounds, temperature charts, bicycles in the air, husband in boxers and mumbles of Psalm 113:9 in my sleep. Yet, nothing—nada, zero, zilch. Oh, wait—something did happen. Suddenly I couldn't walk into a McDonalds or church without weeping, heart twisting at the sight of babies, kids or moms-to-be. Trust me, it got real ugly—anger at God, anger at pregnant women and anger at myself for being angry. I felt awful, but not from morning sickness—it was jealousy, anger, bitterness and despair that had me ready to throw up.

So I counseled with a pastor's wife known for infertility ministry. Apparently many women she counseled/laid hands on became pregnant soon after, so I thought—why not? Since I'm a big believer in prayer, healing and last resorts, I gave it a shot. November came and went, December did too, and then January took me down for the count. I still remember sobbing in church, on my knees with a hard, bitter feeling where a baby should have been. "Why won't you give me a baby, God?" I cried, anger spilling out along with my tears.

Never will I forget the words that drifted in my brain that day, drowning out my sobs, crying babies, the band and the choir:

> *Are you going to throw away this year like you did*
> *with the last?*
> *With bitterness, jealousy and doubt?*
> *Or are you going to lay it and the baby down*
> *and live in peace, hope and faith?*

Ouch. But God got my attention, and I started sobbing again, only this time it was with a repentant and obedient heart. I told God I was sorry and that I would trust Him with the desire of my heart—children—whether it meant biological, adopted or foster. I started praising Him in the face of my infertility because I knew I had the best insurance policy around in Romans 8:28:

And we know that all things (even infertility) work for good for those who love God (love equals obedience, John 14:15) and are called according to His purpose (to glorify Him, Isaiah 43:7).

Every time I saw a mother or mother-to-be after that, I'd rebuke jealousy in Jesus' name and pray, asking God to bless her. Three weeks later my brother waltzed up at a family wedding and said, "Guess what—three weeks of trying and we're pregnant."

Not hello, how are you, or kiss my feet.

Jealousy sprang up like the fountain in the foyer, and I dragged my sister to the bathroom. "Pray with me," I begged, and we did. That God would bless my sister-in-law with

Winner of ACFW's 2009 Debut Author of the Year and 14 RWA awards, **JULIE LESSMAN** is the author of A Passion Most Pure, A Passion Redeemed, A Passion Denied, and A Hope Undaunted, ranked #5 on Booklist's Top 10 Inspirational Fiction for 2010. She and her husband have two children.

a safe and healthy pregnancy and that God would help me to bless her, some way, somehow. That very night I asked her if I could give her a baby shower. She said *yes*! And you know what? So did God— ten months later when my baby was born two months after hers! Go ahead, call it coincidence, but I gotta tell ya right now—this is one mommy who will never buy it!

●

The Old Iron Bed

My Grandma Nora's bed was valuable. It wasn't antique; it wasn't even solid wood. Just painted iron with a wood-grain finish. But it brought high bids around our house.

Grandma came to live with my parents before I was born. Growing up, my sister and I constantly vied for the privilege of sleeping with Grandma in the old iron bed. We'd fight, she'd beg, I'd cry. Because sleeping in Grandma's room wasn't only an honor – it was an adventure!

My grandmother had a nightly routine that rarely varied. After taking off her glasses, she would turn off the bedside lamp. Then a series of strange sounds would commence. A plop, plop then a fizz, fizz followed by some strange clicking, sucking sounds. Finally with a kerploosh, Grandma would roll into bed minus her dentures.

No matter the season, Grandma always slept with the window wide open. One summer morning, I awoke to the neighbor's horse munching outside on freshly planted petunias. One extremely cold January, my father left several cases of Pepsi in Grandma's room to chill. In the middle of the night, her frightened screams brought everyone running as caramel-colored geysers erupted all over her room.

However, no matter how freezing the temperature, the old iron bed remained toasty warm. My nose might be blue with cold, but the rest of my body stayed warm. There was no need for an electric blanket. Not when you had Grandma and six blankets piled high.

She was the very best kind of grandma: The squishy kind. I loved to lay my head on her ample stomach as we'd settle in for the night. She'd run her fingers through my hair and tell me stories about the apple orchards she grew up in and about the day she first saw Grandpa.

Only eighteen at the time, she fell in love at the sight of his shoes. Before seeing the rest of him, some kind of podiatric chemistry caused her to declare to her mother, "I'm going to have those feet under my kitchen table someday!" Three months later she did.

Grandma would stroke my head and tell me about growing up on Washington's Pacific Ocean coast and the adventures of clamming in the moonlight. I could almost hear the sea as I pressed my ear against her stomach. It sounded like the large pink conch shell that sat on the toilet tank in her bathroom. A symphony of marvelous gurgles and mysterious bubbles accompanied her nightly stories.

But best of all, Grandma would pray. After reciting the Lord's Prayer with her and "now I lay me down to sleep," I would snuggle close as she began lifting up family and friends in a low, monotone liturgy of love. Her prayer would start locally and then spread across the world to missionaries, naming them one by one. I can't tell you how Grandma ended her prayers. I was usually asleep by then.

Grandma's old iron bed was the safest place I knew. She didn't have boogeymen under her bed or monsters in her closet. Best of all, she didn't stick her feet in my ribs as my sister was known to do.

As I got older, the overnight rendezvous' became less frequent—especially after Grandma moved into her own apartment. But those repeated stories and bedtime prayers became mooring lines that kept me safe and close when the storms of adolescence threatened to tip my boat.

Grandma passed away when I was just twenty-three. My sister has Grandma's iron bed now. It holds a place of honor in her guest room. Sometimes, when I'm visiting, I cuddle in its embrace with my own children. Telling them about Grandma Nora and apple orchards. Love stories and clamming in the moonlight. Stroking their hair and holding them close until they fall asleep as I pray over them.

Just like Grandma prayed over me.

. . . .

JOANNA WEAVER is known the world over for her transparent and life-changing books, Having A Mary Heart in a Martha World, Having a Mary Spirit and Lazarus Awakening. Her books have sold over a million copies and have been translated into several languages. Joanna is a highly sought after speaker and shares her message at intimate gatherings and several high profile events each year. But Joanna's greatest joy is found in being a wife and mother and her role as a pastor's wife. http://www.joannaweaverbooks.com

Letting Go

I propelled pieces of fruit around my plate. keeping my fork busy without going beyond my sated appetite. Beside me, my son cleaned up the last of his eggs, French toast, and bacon, with a side of muesli and yogurt. If nothing else, I could see that Pat was eating well at college; another reminder that, yes, he could survive on his own quite well.

Our breakfast was the end of Parents' Weekend, a first for us. I had been on the campus of his college since Friday afternoon. Now, at midday on Sunday, things were winding down. Soon, I would be hitting the road for the ride home.

From the day I dropped him off at kindergarten, we had been moving toward this moment. For him, it was one continuous journey of academic, social, and emotional preparation. For me, it was peeling my white-knuckled fingers off him and his life. I still bear the faint line from the caesarian section that brought him into the world; I feared that letting him claim his place out there would leave a much larger incision right where my heart used to be.

And yet, as we approached the start of this new and exciting phase of his life, I felt a shift like mild labor pains. It was time. This child needed to be birthed again, not out of body, but out of the cocoon of his existence with me.

During those first few days and weeks apart, I braced myself for homesickness on his part and separation anxiety on mine, but it never occurred. Surprisingly, we both moved easily and naturally into bigger phases of our own lives: him at college and me deeper into my next writing project. Over the course of eighteen years together, we had both grown to the point that we needed more space in our lives. He quickly flew away from me; I stepped aside and willingly let him go.

Spending the better part of parents' weekend together was fun for me. The best part was when we walked back to the campus together, just the two of us, talking in a way that we hadn't before. Yes, we are still mother and son, but our conversation took on new and shared dimensions as adults and fellow writers. I saw more than my son beside me; I also saw the man he had become.

Late the next morning, we ate a final meal together in the student dining room. With his plate empty and my fruit finished, we had reached the point of departure.

"So, are you ready for me to go home?" I asked.

His shoulders heaved with a huff of a laugh and a smirk twisted his mouth into a mischievous grin. "Yeah, I am."

I waited a moment for the pang, but there was no pain. None at all. "Actually, so am I."

Pat's eyes widened with surprise. A slow blink telegraphed the one-word response he did not have to vocalize. *Really?*

In a split second of silence I asked myself the same question: Are you really ready to leave, to let him go on with his unfolding life here while you return to yours, which is its own work in progress?

PATRICIA CRISAFULLI is a published author of several nonfiction books, including the New York Times Bestseller *The House of Dimon: How JPMorgan's Jamie Dimon Rose to the Top of the Financial World.* She is also the founder of an e-literary magazine, www.FaithHopeandFiction.com.

"Yes," I said aloud, for both our sakes. "It's been great to see you, but it's time to go."

At the car, I hugged and kissed my son good-bye and left, not even looking back, knowing that my eyes had to be on the road before me, while his sought a new direction.

God-Sized Moments

*Our days on earth are like grass; like wildflowers, we
bloom and die.*

(Psalm 103:1, NLT)

A shrill ringing startled me awake at 5 AM, and I immediately knew
who was calling. I stumbled across my pitch-black bedroom,
plopped to the floor, and answered the phone.

"Good morning," came my sister's soft voice, one that sounds so
much like mine, or so we've been told. "Today's the day."

My heart thumped in my chest and I took a deep breath. "When
should I be there?"

We'd known for two years that my sister needed a heart transplant
to survive the long-term damage from chemotherapy and radiation
treatments. Then she'd spent the last five weeks in the hospital,
tethered to the wall and countless monitors.

Each passing day was filled with wondering: Would she get her
new, healthy heart?

And now the day had arrived.

I drove to the hospital, mentally going through all the things in
her room that would need to be packed in preparation for her move
to the ICU after surgery.

The card games that distracted us from the numbers flashing on
monitors.

The food I'd snuck into her room when her sweet tooth kicked in. The get-well cards too numerous to fit on her walls.

Each item came with a memory, and I spent the hours before her transplant sorting and packing, stuffing thoughts and emotions away for a later visit.

Other family members began to arrive, having made the three-hour drive from their homes. And still I worked with focused, robotic-like movements. This was a momentous day—a day of celebration. But also the last day I might share with my sister on earth.

I stayed strong for her six-year-old daughter, desperate to make her smile, making silly faces at her in the hall while straining to hear the surgeon's preparatory words to my sister.

The gurney arrived, and we all crowded around for hugs and kisses. I joined the chorus of family members who spoke words of love and encouragement and then turned toward the waiting room.

Two steps later, I heard my sister's voice. "Where's Sarah?"

Heart in my throat, I stepped away from the others and returned to her, grasping her hand. She squeezed it and said with a shaky voice, "See you on the other side."

I swallowed hard and nodded. No words were necessary…I knew the double meaning. I walked down the sterile white hallway that stretched forever and let my mind wrap around the reality of the moment.

Yes, the Lord was in control. Yes, I believed He'd brought this new heart at the perfect time for my sister. But He could also choose to take her away, to clutch her to His side in heaven and keep her there.

As the day wore on, God reminded me that none of us are guaranteed another day on earth. He brought to mind the small moments He'd allowed me to share with *all* my loved ones.

The times I'd reveled in my daughter's baby-sized giggles.

The memories of sitting at the kitchen table with my four-year-old and teaching him how to play Candy Land.

All those things flooded my thoughts as I heard reports on my sister's progress. "The heart is in," "warming her body temperature back up," "taking longer than expected," "she's stable."

On that life-changing day, the Lord not only gave my sister a new heart, followed by a healthy road to recovery. He also renewed my desire to treasure the gifts I often overlook—those small moments with loved ones that add up to a lifetime of worth.

SARAH FORGRAVE is a novelist who writes contemporary romance from a Christian worldview. A member of American Christian Fiction Writers and Romance Writers of America, Sarah also contributes to the webzine Ungrind. She loves connecting with blog readers on her website, sarahforgrave.com, where she chats about her favorite topics— books, motherhood, and food. When she's not writing, she enjoys being a self-proclaimed fitness nut and stays busy chasing the bundles of energy that live in her Midwest home—her husband and her two young children.

A Princess Tale

Mama was steel magnolia, southern, strong and beautiful, and she taught us as much in her dying as she had in her living. For five years, my mother's Herculean fight introduced me to courage, honor, determination and faith; the kind you find in trenches.

Still, it's not normal for a nine-year-old to lose her mother, and though my father would go on to marry a woman who truly loved me, there remained a hole in my heart. The mother-child bond is *sui generis*...unique. A mother isn't meant to be replaced.

A decade later, I met my husband. Five years after that, we married.

The Lord brought me into a family that had prayed for me since I was six years old. In-laws who loved me fiercely before they even knew my name.

I was gifted with a mother-in-law who held her first born son with open hand, who erred on the side of caution when offering advice (even solicited), esteemed our marriage...and unconditionally loved me as a daughter.

Between hearing friends' dreadful stories of their in-law relationships and having suffered the loss of my mother, I did not take his parents, Tommy and Sarah, for granted. They made it easy to love them back.

Three years after the birth of my first daughter, Sarah came to me with a proposition. She began tentatively, "Would you be interested in hosting a mother-daughter Valentine tea party?" She became increasingly animated as she explained her vision. *We can do this year after year...the girls can dress up and practice good manners...when Rachel turns sixteen, it can be a Sweet Sixteen, her first boy-girl party...*The lady had some crazy ideas. How could I say no?

And so began our annual Valentine tradition.

Those first years were punctuated in splashes of red and pink--from the balloon decor to the glittery Valentine cards we made for the daddies. When the girls were older, we became service-minded and used the opportunity to collect baby items for those in need. We'd circle up and read heartfelt stories that reflected the holiday, themes of friendship, other-mindedness, love.

As each one of my younger brother-in-laws eventually married and had daughters, the party moved from my home to my mother-in-law's, and it became a girls-only tradition in our family (giving up any silly notion for a Sweet Sixteen girl-boy party).

Some things changed. Each cousin invited her very best friend and her mother. Party fare matured, evolving into a sophisticated brunch. Gorgeous flower arrangements replaced balloons.

Some things remained the same. Sunday best, in manners and dress. *Surcies*--little love gifts--given as favors for mother and daughter.

Could my mother-in-law have known when she first asked that she was creating a heritage we would revere for the rest of our lives?

We've continued our Valentine Tea for sixteen years. Through it all, Sarah has honored the women in our family, not for selfish gain but for the glory of God. She has lived the truth of 1 Corinthians 13 in a way that honored her King and taught her children and her children's children well.

She has loved me as a mother loves her children.

Sarah's name means princess.

Fitting, don't you think?

Sarah's example and intention has made a tangible difference in my life as a wife, a mother and a friend. She has taught me the value of tradition, not for tradition's sake but as a manifestation of her faith and to bridge generations.

· ·

In a decades-old, scandalous affair with her husband, Robin also confesses mad crushes on her three teens. As Southern as sugar-shocked tea, she's a recovering people pleaser who advocates talking to strangers. A memoirist, Compassion International Blogger, and Maker-upper of words, Robin writes for her own site, PENSIEVE, and also for (in) courage by DaySpring (a subsidiary of Hallmark) and Simple Mom. She loves to get to know readers through their blog comments and on Twitter and Pinterest. www.pensieve.me

Which compels me to consider the same thing for my children and my children's children. What about you?

Are you on a "Trip to Holland?"

Emily Perl Kingsley's poem was pasted on my refrigerator for the first three years of my son's life. It was titled, *Welcome to Holland.* In essence, it was a snapshot of what it is like to being unprepared when you give birth to a child who has challenges, such as medical or cognitive disabilities.

There is one section of the poem that I read over and over again.

> *After months of eager anticipation, the day finally arrives. You pack your bags and off you go. Several hours later, the plane lands. The stewardess comes in and says, 'Welcome to Holland.' 'Holland?!?' you say.'What do you mean Holland?? I signed up for Italy! I'm supposed to be in Italy. All my life I've dreamed of going to Italy.' But there's been a change in the flight plan. They've landed in Holland and there you must stay.*

My husband and I wanted to go to Italy and ended up in Holland on February 7, 1992. I should have known that our trip to second-time parenthood would be bumpy as we were told that our second born was to be a girl. "Two girls, so nice," my OB-GYN told me. Guess what, we had the first boy born in twenty-eight years in my family when he arrived via emergency c-section. Not breathing right. Sugar too low, heartbeat too high. I could already feel the plane veer off course.

Days later we were allowed to go home only to notice that our little fella was turning the color of a Sunkist orange. Not good. Not good at all. Rushed back to the hospital to be told it was simple jaundice. Nope, nothing in the child's life would be simple, I found out. Days went on, and before the first actual tulip bloomed that year we were in intensive care with our young guy. Jaundice ended up to be a liver problem – not yet determined, but possibly very serious and could lead to severe retardation. RSV nearly claimed his life. Reflux choked him every third breath. Our nightmare continued. You know you have a very sick baby when you can't find room in the isolated PICU suite because of the number of doctors, nurses and respiratory therapists working with your child to keep him alive. You also know your baby is very ill when the nurses come and ask you questions such as, "Is there anyone we can call for you?" Does God have a hotline, I wondered? It was the power of prayer that got us through the darkest days.

For any new parent who has a sick baby you know this is the worst part of the scenario-- waiting. You wait to see if the tests are positive for illnesses that are unimaginable. You wait to see if the insurance will cover the rare and complicated blood work, machines that are helping your child stay alive or special therapy sessions ordered. You wait to see if you will ever have a "normal" life again for yourself, your family, your work. Will your child walk, talk, eat normally, have friends? You begin truly *hate* Holland. And you continue to pray that the nightmare will end.

Then little by little the waiting ends. Test results come

LOUISE MASIN SATTLER is a School Psychologist, Owner of SigningFamilies.com, contributor to Education.com JustAsk column, and a founding member of 411Voices.com. Most importantly she is blessed with a wonderful and healthy husband and grown children. Feel free to connect with Louise at info@SigningFamilies.com back. Therapies begin. Hospitalizations end and you go home. But, for many of us, this is when you start a new journey in to the realm of Special Education. I am here to tell you that there are many caring people in the world to help you on this journey. From doctors, to special educators, to the kindness of neighborhood parents. Our little fella is now a young man. And we love Holland and him more each day.

A Merry Heart

Sometimes family is really all you need. This was reinforced to me when my mother shared a story about her mother, my grandma. You see, when Grandma was a very young girl, around age ten, she was diagnosed with polio. This meant long hospital stays, extremely limited interaction with children her own age and lonely days staring out the window from her hospital bed. In those days, with polio, they felt keeping the children very subdued and quiet was best, and this particular hospital was as drab as could be.

It was also during the time of the Depression, which meant money was tight and life was tough. Day in and day out, she was given the best medicine and treatment, but she wasn't thriving and recovering. Daily visits from adult doctors and specialists are not exactly stimulating for a young girl. Her health was so poor that at one point, a Catholic Priest had administered the "last rites" at her bedside.

One day, her older brother and sister decided to sneak some brand new baby kittens into her hospital room. Their cat Fitzy had just had babies, and the cute kittens were small enough to put in a basket. Upon entering her room, they quietly took off the lid and showed my grandma the sweet little kittens and let her cuddle with them. Great-Grandma saw her mood instantly lift. Her eyes sparkled and she squealed with delight at the cute kitties! Her whole demeanor changed and she came to life.

My Great Grandma took all this in and made a decision that day. She decided that my Grandma would heal much better at home. She promptly checked my Grandma out of the hospital and brought her home with her family. My Grandma did gradually recover, among the love and warmth of her family. You know what Proverbs 17 says: "A merry heart does good like a medicine." I can imagine that she healed emotionally and physically and spiritually as well, and that combined strength wouldn't have been possible in the hospital.

When they left that day, the hospital instructed my Great Grandmother to massage my Grandma's legs every day, something she promised the hospital she would do, and she did. My Grandma was one of the few people we know who did not have a limp or shortened leg due to polio. And perhaps most importantly, the entire family was always praying for my Grandma.

I'm not saying that medicine is bad or unnecessary. But there is no cure quite like the warmth of your family. It's like milk, it simply does a body good. As a pregnant mom about to give birth to a baby boy, I am inspired to provide this same love to my child. May he feel the same warm love from his family that my Grandma felt from hers.

And in this same way, we are called sons and daughters of God.

"But when the fullness of the time had come, God sent forth His Son, born of a woman, born under the law, to redeem those who were under the law, that we might receive the adoption as sons. And because you are sons, God has sent forth the Spirit of

MEGAN ALEXANDER can be seen nightly as a television correspondent for the top rated news magazine show Inside Edition. She also appears on the CNN program Showbiz Tonight. She especially enjoys reporting on stories with a heart. She graduated from Westmont College with a degree in Political Science. She loves speaking to youth and works with Girls Inc. and National American Miss. She and her husband reside in the New York City area and attend Redeemer Church of Manhattan. For more on Megan, go to www.meganalexander.com. Megan's mother, Mary, resides in Seattle and provided insight into this essay. Follow Megan on twitter : @meganalexander1

His Son into your hearts, crying out, "Abba, Father!" Therefore you are no longer a slave but a son, and if a son, then an heir of God through Christ." (Galatians 4:4-7)

God claims you and me as his children. This is a wonderful gift and identity that is good for our heart and soul, and something that is more powerful than all the medicine in the world.

SUZANNE WOODS FISHER

What is a Grandmother?

"A grandmother is a little bit parent, a little bit teacher,
and a little bit best friend."

—*Amish proverb*

I arrived late in the night in Rhode Island, anxious to meet my two-day-old grandson, Blake, after a full day of flying. My daughter and son-in-law had just returned home from the hospital and felt like they had been in a train wreck. There was stuff everywhere. Already, the needs of this little eight-pound bundle of joy were enormous: an all-terrain stroller, plenty of diapers, onesies, spit-up rags, an assortment of pacifiers to try out until he found the ideal one.

And he was perfect.

I know, I know. "Every mother crow thinks her own little crow is the blackest." But this little dark eyed, dark haired boy really was perfect.

I spent the next seven days and nights getting to know this little guy. His schedule (he had none), his hunger cries (very similar to his every other cry). His pirate look--one eye open, one eye squeezed shut, as if he was still surprised by all that had taken place to him in a week's time.

I felt surprised, too. How could my baby possibly have had a baby? How could I be a grandmother? I had just turned fifty-one. Shockingly young! How could a kid like me give up playing tennis three times a week to settle into knitting and crocheting and Friday night bingo? And shouldn't I alter my appearance to fit this new label? Give up my jeans? Switch over to below knee-length calico dresses, thick black socks, practical shoes, gray hair pinned in a topknot. Think...Aunt Bee on Mayberry R.F.D.

As soon as people knew my daughter was expecting, I was bombarded with advice from my well-meaning friends—even those who weren't yet grandparents. "The best way to avoid getting on the nerves of your daughter and son-in-law is to not say anything. Ever." Or "You'd better pick your nickname or you'll be stuck with something hideous, like MooMoo Cow."

· · · · · · · · · · · · · · · · · · · ·

SUZANNE WOODS FISHER is the bestselling novelist of The Keeper and The Choice, as well as nonfiction books about the Amish, including Amish Values for Your Family and Amish Proverbs. Her interest in the Anabaptist cultures can be directly traced to her grandfather, W. D. Benedict, who was raised in the Old Order German Baptist Brethren Church in Franklin County, Pennsylvania. Benedict eventually became publisher of Christianity Today magazine. Suzanne is the host of a radio show called Amish Wisdom and her work has appeared in many magazines. She lives in California. www.suzannewoodsfisher.com

What should I be called? Granny? No...reminded me of The Beverly Hillbillies. Grandma? No...sounded like The Waltons. Grammy? No...it was already taken by the in-laws.

But no one really explained what it meant to be a grandmother. I didn't know myself, not until I held baby Blake in my arms. In that moment, I realized that he was one of mine. He belongs to me. He will be on my mind and in my prayers, every day, for the rest of my life. There's a bond between us that can't be broken. He has altered my life forevermore.

I had become a grandmother.

TRICIA GOYER

Adoption: a Mother's Greatest Gift

I held the small baby in my arms, wrapped up in a receiving blanket to keep her warm from the chill of the delivery room, and a voice spoke to me. "Congratulations, Mom."

The congratulations came from an unlikely source--the grandmother of this child, the mother of the sweet birth mother who chose adoption for her baby girl.

To say I was overwhelmed is an understatement. Thankfulness filled my heart--to God, who'd answered my prayers, and to the birth mom who'd chosen our family for her daughter. I also ached that my joy would be another's heartache. Working with teen moms for ten years, I was often an advocate for the young mother. I knew that while the weeks and months ahead would be a time of celebration for our family, they would be ones of heartache and grieving for this woman.

Adoption is a wonder and the beauty, and the sacrifice of it is never so clear as on Mother's Day. My new daughter is one year old now, and she is a huge part of my heart. Her life is a gift to my days, and her smile can make even the most dreary afternoon bright. I can honestly say there is no difference in the love I feel between her and my three other children. If anything the love feels even more special because she was an unexpected gift. John and I learned about her just two and a half months prior to her being born. The years of prayers to expand our family were answered quickly and beautifully.

The sacrifice of adoption makes my heart ache, for I know on this Mother's Day another woman will be thinking about my daughter—her daughter. As I rejoice, I'll be crying tears for her. I'll also be sending up prayers that God will wrap His arms around her in a special way.

This Mother's Day, I cannot help but think about Christ's sacrifice to make our adoption into God's family possible. Maybe it's because just a few weeks ago we were celebrating Easter, but I'm reminded anew that my gain required His loss, His pain. The greatest love, it seems, is not shown with flowers, chocolate or a diamond bracelet. The greatest love is shown when, because of your love for another, your desires and comfort are laid down for the greater good of someone else.

As Ephesians 1:3 says, *"How blessed is God! And what a blessing he is! He's the Father of our Master, Jesus Christ, and takes us to the high places of blessing in him. Long before he laid down earth's foundations, he had us in mind, had settled on us as the focus of his love, to be made whole and holy by his love. Long, long ago he decided to adopt us into his family through Jesus Christ. (What pleasure he took in planning this!) He wanted us to enter into the celebration of his lavish gift-giving by the hand of his beloved Son"* (The Message).

. . . .

TRICIA GOYER is a CBA best-selling novelist of 35 novels and the winner of two American Christian Fiction Writers' Book of the Year Awards (Night Song and Dawn of a Thousand Nights). She co-wrote 3:16 Teen Edition with Max Lucado and contributed to the Women of Faith Study Bible. Tricia is the host of a weekly radio show Living Inspired. Also a noted marriage and parenting writer, she lives with her husband and children in Arkansas. You can connect with Tricia at www.triciagoyer.com.

Perhaps you know an adoptive mother. Take time this Mother's Day to let her know that the beauty of her gift is not missed by you. Also, take time to thank God for adopting you into His forever family, thanking Jesus Christ for His sacrifice. I wouldn't be the mother I am without this Gift of Love.

CHERYL WYATT

Gifting With Presence

"...God loves a cheerful giver." (2 Cor. 9:7b, NIV)

I grew up when it was popular for moms to work rather than stay home. I remember the day my parents decided that regardless of this trend in society my mom would stay with us rather than work outside the home. Like today, the economy was terrible. We lived in a uranium mining town and everyone struggled financially. Our family was no different. Our parents sat us down and talked to us about how the decision would change the priorities of our family. They mentioned how Christmases and birthdays would be scaled down gift-wise. As Mom put it, "You kids will have my presence more than my presents."

I admit, as a youngster, that didn't sound so appealing...until I realized how much better I felt with Mom watching us rather than random babysitters who never seemed to love us as much as Mom. Now, as a mom myself, I realize that my fondest memories aren't wrapped up in gifts my parents gave to me but in time they spent with us, from camping trips to day to day chores together.

Have you ever danced with a laundry basket? I have a specific memory of Mom putting a Super Bubble record on and dancing with me during washcloth folding marathons. She made chores more fun, less mundane.

One line in a popular worship song says, "Above all else, give me yourself."

That is a profound song to me because it echoes the prayer of my heart in maintaining closeness with God. Time spent together is *crucial* to relationship. I think it also echoes the cries of many children's hearts in yearning for more time with their parents. I talked to my mom as a teen because she listened to me as a toddler and beyond.

Above all else, give them yourself.

Like Mom, I left my career to stay home with my children. God made a way when there seemed to be no way. Miraculously, we seemed to have as much money when I stayed home as when I was working. My children tell me over and over how much they appreciate that my husband and I take time for them. Just to be with them. To listen. Watch movies together. To engage them in conversation about their day, triumphs, struggles at school, their latest crush or new favorite song. Then we listen to them sing it whether we think we have the time or not.

We've had to sacrifice giving our children things, but they are by no means lacking. As one friend said, "My house may not always be clean, but my children know they're loved."

I long to live like that. Admittedly I am compulsive about cleanliness. I've tried to be creative with chores. For instance— laundry sorting relays. I assign a color to each kid. They scramble to Mount Laundry, grab their colors then run them to their basket. The first one finished wins a prize which can be an extra date with Mom. I give the gift of myself over money. My presence more than my presents. Two commodities that always seem in short demand are time and money. Your children may not realize it now, but later in life the memories that will mean the most are ones in which you spent time. I'm pretty certain when they look back on their life with you, their fondest memories won't be things you got for them, but things you did with them.

How do you give your children the gift of yourself? What things do you do together? I encourage you to share inexpensive family-time ideas with friends.

Born Valentine's Day on a naval base, **RN CHERYL WYATT** writes award-winning military romance. Her Love Inspired debuts earned RT Top Picks plus #1 and #4 on eHarlequin's Top 10 Most-Blogged-About-Books, lists including NYT Bestsellers. Her books have also garnered a Romantic Times Reviewers Choice Award, a Gayle Wilson Award of Excellence final and other awards. For more info, join her newsletter in the space provided at www.CherylWyatt..

AMANDA BENNETT

Make Time for an Encouraging Word

While I have my dad's smile and height, I definitely have my mom's eyes and her gift of encouraging others. I have learned many lessons from my mom, but the importance of encouragement is one of the best.

Growing up in a big family, time with my mom was always at a premium, but there was a constant draw to her side. She has always been the spark in the room and the sought-after listener.

I was at the store recently, and one of the cashiers came to get me to go through her checkout, just so we could talk. I listened to her dilemma about wanting to go back to school, and then offered a few tips and some "you can do this" kinds of encouragement. As I was walking out, one of the managers walked up and asked about Mom, who was out of town. After I explained Mom's absence, the manager smiled and told me how she loved Mom's smile and her kind words of encouragement. *Mirror, mirror, on the wall . . . I am my mother, after all!*

It all started when we were small children. Mom made a point of listening carefully to our stories and ideas, as if every word we said was very important. Then she would talk to us about what was on our minds and have nothing but kind, hopeful words to say to us, making each of us feel like we were the most important thing in her life at that moment. She would always find time to listen, even if it had to be squeezed in during the crazy dinnertime sessions that took place around the table of a widow with four teenagers.

First she would listen, think, and then reassure us with "You can do this," or "You know what you might want to try?" She never said, "That won't work," or "You can't do that." She was always the one to make us believe in ourselves and our dreams. Whether it was a difficult class or teacher, a college application, or a rift in a friendship, she would listen and encourage.

The most prized lesson that Mom taught me was that as a mom, I needed to be the encourager for my children. I didn't fully appreciate the value of the lesson until my children faced those social situations that we all know will come around eventually. As my children grew and blossomed, my role as encourager came to be a natural one.

As they approach adulthood and move on to their own lives, I find that I am still filling the role of encourager and listener. As I listen and talk with them—by phone, email, or text—I have to smile. I hear my mom's sweet voice coming through in my words, and I am so grateful to have her as a part of my life. She is still my most powerful encourager!

I can't begin to explain the peace and assurance that come from that kind of mom, knowing she's there to listen, point out the prickly parts, and then encourage from beginning to end. Offering precious words and thoughts treasured for a lifetime, Mom is still teaching me the lesson of priceless encouragement. Take time to ramp up your encouragement role—there are so many people around who need kind words and a moment of your time and attention. It's a multigenerational investment!

Taking on each day for all it holds, Amanda loves to share her encouraging outlook with humor and honesty. She has a passion for life and living it with great expectation, and she shares this perspective as an author and speaker. As a wife, mom, and daughter, Amanda knows what it is like to fill many roles and meet countless needs. She travels across the country as a speaker and writes from the family farm in Tennessee, high up in the clouds of the Appalachians. www.unitstudy.com.

PAULA MOLDENHAUER

●

Dollars and Doll Houses

I squirmed in the pew as an offering was collected. I was a nine-year-old contemplating a dilemma. I only had one dollar, and didn't know when I could get another. I had no change, nothing but that bill. Surely God didn't want me to give it up! But my little girl heart wanted to be bigger than my selfishness—to trust God with all I had. At the last minute, I dropped the money into the plate.

Later that day, Grandma motioned for me to follow her outside her farmhouse. The screen door creaked as we slipped through, and the coolness of the covered back porch greeted us. "Now you don't need to tell anyone about this," she whispered to me as she slipped a dollar bill into my hand.

I wondered if Grandma knew I'd given all I had at church that day, or if God had prompted her to replace my gift. I took the dollar, wrapped her in a hug, and discovered you can't out-give God.

It was a lesson I'd need often as I matured. There were many times I was prompted to give when I couldn't afford to do so. And there were many times God met needs—and desires—well beyond my husband's and my ability to provide them for our young family.

My daughter Sarah had saved her money for months to buy a doll house, accumulating quite a sum for a four-year-old. As her savings grew, it dawned on me I'd never talked with her about giving to God. I didn't require her to give an offering of her little stash since we hadn't discussed it initially, but I did encourage her to begin developing a lifelong habit of giving back to God a portion of what He blessed her with.

My sweet little girl agonized. I left the decision to her, but told her not to worry—you couldn't out-give God. In the end she dipped into her savings and gave God an offering. She seemed at peace with her decision, but I saw the sacrifice in her eyes as she pulled the bills from her bank.

A few days later our neighbors moved unexpectedly. Left-behind toys were heaped in front of the house for the garbage collector, and a friend noticed a treasure in the pile. We grabbed Sarah's hand and ran up the block. There sat a perfect dollhouse trimmed in pink siding, with a little button in the nursery that, when pushed, lit up the room and played a lullaby.

When we reached to pick up the dollhouse, Sarah pointed to several items next to it: a couple of dolls, a fancy pink convertible, and dollhouse furniture. The three of us loaded the treasures into our arms. It didn't take long to sanitize the toys, and then Sarah and I rushed to the store where she spent her savings to finish furnishing the dollhouse.

Sarah could never have afforded all the items given to her that day. We both knew they were God's special gift of love to her.

God freely gives us everything—salvation, eternity, and wonder of wonders, Himself. We could never give enough to tip the balance in our favor. But He taught us to hold our money a little more loosely by showing us He not only saw our meager sacrifices, but could be trusted with the desires of our hearts.

Just as I never forgot the dollar God gave back to me through my grandmother, Sarah's behavior as a generous adult shows me she hasn't forgotten the lesson of the doll house. In her new world of adult responsibilities, where cars need gas and insurance, food doesn't miraculously appear, and money doesn't grow on trees, she is still a generous person. You can't out-give God.

Author, speaker and mom of four, **PAULA MOLDENHAUER** longs to be close enough to Jesus to breathe His fragrance. Published over 300 times, Paula's first book, You're a Charmer, Mr. Grinch, releases in 2012. Visit her: www.paulamoldenhauer.com

SHELLEY MALCOLM

"No One You-er Than You"

A Masterpiece Under Construction

Years of old class photographs reflect the real deal. I was the one with the tilted horn-rimmed glasses with sparkles in the corners. I had the smile with crowded teeth, which could actually cut a perfect letter "M" into an apple, until they eventually surrendered to silver wires and brackets. My hair was never without crooked bangs and untamed cowlicks.

Occasionally, I would think of what it might be like to be one of the popular and pretty girls who seemed more graceful and privileged. They took lessons in something called "Class" (which of course, meant it must be something I did not have). I also wondered what it might be like to not be so shy, and to live in a family whose father had not died.

Fortunately, my mother modeled optimism and hope through heartbreak, and love grounded in faith. She taught some profound truths: "Be yourself . . . it is too hard to try to be like someone else for very long. Being yourself is something you will do better than anyone else."

> *"Today you are you! That is truer than true! There is*
> *no one alive that is You-er than You!"*
> *-Dr. Suess, Happy Birthday to You!*

100

The words of Dr. Suess seem simple and silly, yet in them I hear not only my mom's voice, but even an echo of God's great love, as in Psalm 139.

> *"For you created my inmost being: you knit me together in my mother's womb. I praise you, because I am fearfully and wonderfully made: Your works are wonderful, l know that full well. My frame was not hidden from you when I was made in that secret place. When I was woven together in the depths of the earth your eyes saw my unformed body. All the days ordained for me were written down in your book before one of them came to be."* Psalms 139:1316

We can't deny the origins of our heritage, nor those threads that will weave through future generations. This is our fingerprint for life, the basic ingredient for the work-in progress that is you or me.

The words of my mother, Dr. Suess, and the psalmist meant even more to me when I became a mother of four. They're an affirmation of the miracle that is a human being. How can we love each child less than unconditionally? We are called to not favor or compare one to another, but love each one as the extraordinary individual they are born to be. You may think you have no gifts or little talent. It is certain, however, that God has not forgotten them. They will not be "hidden under a bushel;" they'll be revealed at an unexpected time under unanticipated circumstances.

> *"Which can say more than this rich praise? That you alone are you."* Wm Shakespeare, Sonnet 84

Another part of my mom's advice was to "Like your own company," which meant to celebrate the person that we see in the mirror. Shakespeare's words sound so empowering, yet it can be uncomfortable and difficult to understand the blessing in the darkest days when we feel alone. Yet it's exactly those wounds and scars, failures and mistakes, losses and sorrows that turn a grain of sand into a pearl. These experiences are the fires that forge the finest steel.

> *"Be joyful always; pray continually; give thanks in all circumstances, for this is God's will for you in Jesus Christ."* 1 Thessalonians 5:16

Paul's words tell us to be thankful for the all of the adventure that is our own life story. My mother, Eileen, now at age ninety-one, stands fast and fearless in her faith, like you and like me—a masterpiece under construction.

SHELLEY MALCOLM is the author of "REAL", a collection of 60 inspirational stories with photos by Terilee Dawn Ouimette. Shelley Malcolm was named Pismo Beach's Citizen of the Year in 2011 for her extensive contributions and involvement in the community. Proceeds from her book will benefit the Alzheimer's Foundation and other charities. Shelley Malcolm resides in Shell Beach, California with her husband, Doug. For more information, please visit http://marthamartha.net.

SARAH WAUTERLEK

"My Mother-In-Love"

Recently I was asked what I want truly want in life and after deflecting the question, the man with whom I was speaking slowly leaned forward on his chair and with great intensity, asked the same question again. At that moment I knew that he wasn't going to let me go with giving him an answer that satisfied. And so, as his eyes bore deep into mine and we sat there in that uncomfortable silence, thoughts and emotions swirled around in my head until they formed what I believed to be a cohesive and honest answer. I simply said, "I want there to be purpose."

My Mother In-Law, or Mother In-Love as I had learned to call her, is someone who demonstrates great purpose in her life. She works tirelessly for her family, for those around her, and most importantly, for the less fortunate of the world. Since establishing Hands of Hope, she has effectively changed the lives of not only the poor in Africa, but also the lives of the wealthy in America. She has demonstrated that we are all created for purpose and that we can all do something that gives back and makes a difference. We are all unique pieces of a puzzle that when brought together create something beautiful and of value.

Vicky has brought me to Africa three times and on every trip I have felt tremendous blessing and challenge. It has been a blessing to see first hand the work that her non-profit, Hands of Hope, is doing on the ground in Africa. My soul is filled with joy when I see the smiling faces of the children who now attend school or the pride that is exhibited by those who have received micro-finance loans and now are able to provide for their families. I am overcome with happiness when I see the gratitude of those who have clean water because of wells that have been built or because of the money they can now earn from the chickens and goats that they have been given. Hands of Hope has done tremendous work in not only feeding the poor, but in teaching them how to be self- sufficient. There is a newly found purpose to their lives and also to ours here in America. I have seen with my own eyes how we can all work together to make a difference and have always felt challenged by it, as I know many have.

Vicky's giving heart, coupled with her wise and clever mind, makes her effective in all that she does. I have silently watched as she has single handedly accomplished more than one woman is expected. Some would say it comes effortlessly, but I have seen her efforts and the time she puts into her work. She has shown me, without words, how to persist. She has shown me how to leverage what you are given to accomplish more for those in need and she has encouraged me to do so whether it is with my photography, my travel business, or in seemingly unimportant every day interactions with those I meet. Every day, every moment, and every effort can count.

Vicky and I have experienced the best and the worst of life together. We have experience great joy and now, unfortunately, we have experienced great pain in the loss of her son, and my husband, Mark. Since Mark's death Vicky and I have traveled back to Africa together and in the midst of our heartache, our sense of purpose on this earth was renewed. Our hearts were broken after losing Mark and slowly, in giving back, they are healing. I have found that the heart may break and bend and bleed and throb. However, the heart endures. The heart can mend. The heart can heal in time. Sometimes the love that we lost can morph into something new and beautiful that helps us to move forward with renewed strength and vision. Sometimes you can see streams of light in even the darkest of places. May love lost increase the capacity for new love to be experienced. Prayers for the heart to feel again do not discount the love it once felt. Instead it honors it for love lost has prepared the heart to feel more, love more, and be more.

Sarah is a travel enthusiast, photographer, runner, foodie, writer, teacher, adventure seeker, lover of laughter, lover of people, and lover of life. Raised in Minnesota, having spent five years in Chicago, she now currently resides in Los Angeles when not traveling the globe. She is the co-founder of Traveler's Gift Vacations (www.travelersgiftvacations.com) and founder of Sarah Wauterlek Photography (www.sarahwauterlekphotography.com). She is the author of the book, Young Widow: A Memoir.

CINDI FERRINI

Pearls of Promise

They made a promise to each other: "Our family will not be the same way ours was when we were growing up in our families." There were areas in the lives of my parents that they did not want repeated. The word "alcohol" should conjure up enough thoughts for us to realize they wanted different. They wanted better. They promised. They kept that promise for over fifty-one years.

As a recipient of that promise, my siblings and I benefited by having my parents at *every* event in which the four of us participated: sports, music, school related functions, church. They made us a priority and we knew it.

At the end of my senior year of high school, Mom was recovering from varicose vein surgery on both legs. She was limited to walking certain distances for a time. It was Parent's Night at our last football game - seniors welcomed their parents to escort them on the field to be introduced. I thought Dad might join me alone, but there was Mom, walking slow, but standing tall with us. I couldn't help wonder, even at that time, if she was excited to be doing something she never got to do—having dropped out of school in the tenth grade so she could work to help provide for the family.

Dad was often on the road as a business owner, but I don't recall him not being at an event. Maybe I'm forgetting, but if that's so, love covered the times he missed being there. He wasn't the type to gush with hugs and kisses, but was often heard to say, "I'm so proud of you," something I don't think he heard much as an eight-year-old from his widower dad.

That promise they made to each other was really to us kids, too. We enjoyed a good, healthy, and stable childhood. Both of my parents, and my husband's, were there to welcome each of our children to the world. They helped take care of all the kids, and often cared for our son with special needs so we could get a break, engage in ministry, or visit with friends freely. And for a long while, they came to many of our children's events.

When they marked their last year together, Mom and the three of us daughters remaining had cared for Dad for over six years as he continued a downhill spiral with strokes, Alzheimers, rehab, and hospital stays. Then Mom suffered a massive heart attack in a restaurant, eating alone while a caregiver stayed with Dad.

Left on life support, Mom was not going to last much longer. Dad, barely able to gather lucid thoughts very much, said clearly, "I want to see my bride." Into his wheelchair and to the hospital we took him – my sister placing Mom's hand in his. Mom was not conscious, and Dad said not a word. We wept, knowing their promise was coming to an end.

Mom passed away five days after her heart attack. Dad slipped away five days later.

The beauty of the love we experienced growing up transferred into their care and love for each other when it wasn't easy. Now we're left to carry on that promise. Our job isn't done yet, but because of the example we had, we're off to a good start.

When I learn of someone who's tried to "do it right," I don't think of it as pressure for us to do it their way, but an encouragement to pursue promises for our own families. Our promises will look different from those of our parents, but if the Lord is in the center of it all—it will be precious. That's a promise that will be a pearl!

CINDI FERRINI is the co-author with her husband Joe of Unexpected Journey: When Special Needs Change Our Course, and the author of Balancing the Active Life (bible study), and Get It Together-an organizational planner, as well as a conference speaker, artist, mother of three and grandmother. To find out more or contact Cindi visit her website: www.cindiferrini.com.

Gift Giving

My mother had what you could call a unique style of gift giving, the value of which was often lost on her young adult children. She didn't care much about formalities. At Christmas, it was not uncommon for my mother to hand us a box that was wrapped in tinfoil instead of paper, or taped with mailing labels instead of Scotch tape. Sometimes I might receive a very well-wrapped gift, but with a numbered label instead of my name. She explained this was so we would not guess which gift was for whom—only to forget which number she had assigned to each kid.

She would smile and shrug her shoulders. "I'm not quite sure if this is yours...it may be for your brother."

I would open the box to find an economy size package of men's sweat socks.

"Oops!" She would take the package from my hands and present it to my brother with the same amount of flourish and enthusiasm.

I know now that her gifts were just one example of the kind of mother that she was. Nurturing, caring, expecting her children to be kind and generous more than proper or organized. She wanted to make others around her feel good about themselves and taken care of, and she showed this through her many comical acts of thoughtfulness.

After a series of small strokes, my mother had a large one. The stroke left her unable to walk and needing twenty-four-hour care.

Reluctantly, we made arrangements for a nursing home and began the painful process of packing up her house.

When I went into her linen closet, I found boxes and boxes of unopened lotion bottles. I pulled out the colorful bottles and recognized many of them, her favorite brands and sets that would often surface as birthday gifts or in care packages. Exasperated, I asked, "How dry is your skin?"

"I collect them," she responded indignantly.

"Mom, people collect coins, or books, or figurines, not lotion bottles."

I did not know then that she had spent all year stockpiling to give gifts to her children, nieces, and friends, that she might not be there one day to hand them out.

My mother died on a freezing cold February morning. I was twenty-seven years old. I had gotten used to the unpredictability of strokes. But after a few days in the ICU, she did not wake up. A young doctor quietly told us that she had passed.

My brothers and I sat in the waiting room, nodding as we took the information in. A bag of fresh muffins sat on the table. My brother had brought them to give to the doctors and nurses. We packed up what was left her of belongings and began the long and complex experience of adjusting to life without her.

A year and a half later, when my daughter was born, all I could see in her small, calm face was my own mother's. As we drove home, I cried, feeling so lucky and sad at the same time. I wished my mother could be waiting for me. Next to me were all the gifts I would have longed for, beautiful blankets and tiny baby outfits, but I wondered what practical items I would need in the middle of the night. My mother would have made sure we had them.

As life goes on, I find myself pulling out all of those things that she had given us, things we had laughed at. A fleece winter hat that can be converted to cover almost the entire face—it went to a football game with my husband in sub-zero temperatures. A do-it-all blender ended up being used to make baby food. The very last bottle of almond scented lotion in what had once seemed like an endless supply in my vanity cabinet.

Her true gifts, the ones that came wrapped in tinfoil and wrongly labeled boxes, were the things she always hoped to provide: the reassurance that her children would always be safe and taken care of, that we would have everything that we needed. This is the lesson she left with me: to care for ourselves and those who depend on us, long after she is gone.

BETH CANNING LUPO works with birth parents at The Cradle, an adoption agency in Evanston, Illinois. She attended Boston University as an undergraduate and went on to receive a Masters degree in Psychology from Northwestern University. Beth devotes time to her large extended family and to charitable organizations, including participating on the governing board for Rainbows, a non profit which provides grief support to children. She currently lives in Chicago with her husband and one year old daughter, Charlie.

❦

My Mormor

M*ormor:* In Danish it means my mother's mother. My Mormor was a wife, a mother, and a partner with my Morfar (mother's father) for nearly fifty years. Together they owned a shoe shop in Skaerbaek, a tiny village in Southern Jutland, Denmark. I was always close with my Mormor. When I was very young, my dad was in the FBI, and his duties were dangerous. One of the things that the Bureau worried about was the kidnapping of a high-profile agent's child. So my parents wisely sent me to Skaerbaek to be with my Mormor for some time.

I loved the smell of her cooking -- Danish meatballs, potatoes straight from the ground, and soup with vegetables from her garden. My Mormor didn't speak any English (except for *Hi* and *Goodbye*), so I spoke Danish, rode my bike to the farmer's market for goods, and played cards with her late into the nights.

Later, as a college student, I was blessed with a grant to go to Denmark and interview Freedom Fighters from WWII. My Mormor's stories about the war had ignited a passion in me. I wanted to find out what had happened in this tiny village, in this tiny country. Why had the Danes resisted the Germans? It wasn't just that King Christian wore the Star of David as he rode down the streets of Copenhagen. It was that the entire country had mounted a resistance, a Cold Shoulder (Kuld Skulder) to Nazi oppression. Hitler had thought the Danes, blue eyed and fair haired, would be his allies. They were not. But why? And would anyone talk to me so many years later?

My deft and capable Mormor swung into action. She made coffee, baked cookies, and off we were. Together we interviewed everyone in the village. Me with my little note pad, and my Mormor with her sweet face and probing questions: "Hans, how exactly did you get messages to the British? And did Esther know? Did she approve? Why?" Journalists of today could learn a lesson from my Mormor.

The spirit and passion of those in Skaerbaek will forever fuel my soul. They could have gone the easy route and given in to Nazi promises. They did not, to their own peril.

One night, over a competitive game of cards, my Mormor put her own cards down. She told me about the time shortly after the war was "officially" over. She was cleaning a rug in the back garden and she saw something more than a squirrel. She saw an emaciated young man in a German uniform. She gave him bread, water, and a new pair of shoes from their shop. She recognized that he was some mother's son, some Mormor's grandson.

There is a red and blue arm band that many Freedom Fighters wore. One gave me his over coffee and cookies with my Mormor. I looked to my Mormor. *Should I accept this?* I said with my eyes. She said *yes* with hers. My Mormor was just that way.

LIS WIEHL is a New York Times best-selling author, Harvard Law School graduate, and former federal prosecutor. A popular legal analyst and commentator for the Fox News Channel, Wiehl appears on The O'Reilly Factor and was co-host with Bill O'Reilly on the radio for seven years. Wiehl's fiction includes the bestselling Triple Threat and East Salem novels.

SHARON BITTLE

●

Motherhood

Again he asked, "What shall I compare the kingdom of God to? It is like a yeast that a woman took and mixed into a large amount of flour until it worked all through the dough."

(Luke 13:20, NIV)

During my childhood, mother and I made homemade pizza dough every Friday afternoon. The recipe called for three simple ingredients: flour, yeast, and warm water. Making those pizzas was a special ritual in our house. First of all, it was the one day a week that the six of us looked forward to the same meal, unlike the liver and onions she sometimes surprised us with. Dad worked later on Friday and my older siblings weren't interested in helping mom, so I had her undivided attention in the kitchen. I was a precocious and loquacious child. My mother, now on the seasoned side of motherhood, had developed some clever ways to parent.

Transforming the three ingredients into the delicious dough required no appliances prior to baking, so I could be in charge of the process. We had a certain bowl that mom would retrieve from the cabinet; then I would get to mixing. The next step was to wait for the dough to rise, which had to take place in a warm and quiet environment. So I would march the dough to my parents' bedroom and hide it under a pillow. Then I'd shut the door carefully and tiptoe

113

back to the kitchen to quietly continue with pizza prep work. After some time I was summoned to gather the bowl, bring it to the kitchen, and quietly, playfully knead the dough. Mom inspected my work and the process repeated itself. Sometimes the dough really needed a long, quiet, amount of time before the yeast worked hard enough, according to Mom. I was never quite sure how long it needed, but I was sure quiet, so it worked.

It wasn't until I became a mother myself that I came to truly appreciate peace and quiet. And it wasn't until I became a mother myself that I came to realize my mother's wit and wisdom. Since then, I have been in awe of how God is the ultimate parent. Jesus' parable of the woman and the yeast speaks to me because I learned at an early age, hands-on, how powerful yeast was. It made dough rise and much to my surprise, kept me quiet for an entire Friday afternoon.

SHARON BITTLE is blessed to be a stay-at-home mom, she and her husband Mark have two sons. Sharon would like to thank the pastoral staff at their church for posing the question "How will you know if you are called to do something if you don't even try?" She is a graduate of Northwestern University and in between laundry is trying new things.

When I read Luke and Jesus' description of the kingdom of heaven, I think of a mother's love for her child. Since I know firsthand how powerful that love is, I am in awe of how amazing God's love is for me. God had a plan for me and placed me in my mother's womb long before I became aware of His existence, let alone love. The same way He has a plan for my children. During those motherhood moments where I long for peace and quiet, I pray for God's wisdom to give me the recipe for my individual child. I know that He is the seasoned chef and I am only an assistant in the kitchen of His kingdom.

The Fire-Fighting, Ballet-Teaching Mom

"God can do anything, you know – far more than you could ever imagine or guess or request in your wildest dreams! He does it not by pushing us around but by working within us, his Spirit deeply working gently within us."

(Ephesians 3:20, MSG)

I can remember it like it was yesterday. I was six and in Mrs. Barr's first grade class at Saint Michael's Episcopal School in Dallas, Texas. We were given an assignment to come to school dressed up as what we wanted to be when we grew up. I was thrilled! I couldn't wait to get out of my stiff school uniform and into something much more interesting. I showed up at school in a leotard, tights, ballet slippers, fire fighters hat, and a purse. You see, my dream job at six was to be a fire-fighting, ballet-teaching mom.

At age six, that didn't seem the slightest bit odd. At six, anything seemed possible.

I am thankful my mother didn't even pause at my crazy outfit. She didn't try to convince me that I couldn't be all three things at once. When it came to creativity, in our house the lid was always lifted and the skies were always the limit.

Take a moment and just think about the age of six. You were learning to write sentences, creating art projects that were mini-Picasso paintings, and inventing fascinating lands for your dolls to explore. The world was filled with such potential and you were the creator.

But, like a red T-shirt after forty washes, the vibrancy of our life begins to fade. We slowly but surely become about test scores, matching clothes, fitting in with the cool kids, and eventually focus on the "perfect job" that looks nothing like a fire-fighting, ballet-teaching mom. Somewhere between six and twenty-six, the ideas of creating, imagining, dreaming, adventuring all become at odds with societies' expectations of adulthood.

Yet my mom always kept an incredible example of creativity in front of me: Jesus. Jesus serves as our adult example of how to do life differently. Jesus's approach to life on earth was to generate new ideas and associations over existing concepts. Take a look at His resume: used mud and spit for healing, walked on water, made a storm stop, brought a man back to life, fed five thousand people with two fish and five loaves of bread, and rounding it out by being raised from the dead. Jesus was at constant odds with society's expectations.

My mom always said that my job was to be Christ's hands and feet, which meant we are to imitate what He did on the earth over 2,000 years ago in our present day life. That means you and I are called to be people of creativity.

"For since creation of the world, God's invisible qualities – his eternal power and divine nature - have been clearly seen, being understood from what has been made, so that men are without excuse." Romans 1:20

What is it that you loved to do at the age of six that is missing from your present life? How can you wake up the six-year-old in you that is napping? Whatever that something is, re-discover it! Go buy yourself some paper and finger paints, bubbles, paper dolls. Give yourself permission to return to the land of imagination and wild dreams.

Why? Why bother with that?

Because Christ said so! With some nudges from my mama.

Because you are creative, and inside that creativity lies the ability to shape and mold the world for Christ.

Adulthood may have come, but the adventure never ends.

Encourage creativity in yourself and family. Are you encouraging creativity in those around you by setting the example of what it means to creative in Christ's image?

CAREY BAILEY is a recovering perfectionist, wife, proud mama and Family Life director for her church in Surprise, Arizona. On the side she loves party planning, crafting, and pursuing her dream of writing. She has a degree in religion from Westminster College and writes at her blog found at www.CareyBaileyOnline.com.

ANDREA MULLINS

The Legacy of Forgiveness

If there is one thing I am sure of, it's the unconditional forgiveness of my parents. Regardless of my behavior, my mother and father never quit loving me and always forgave me. In fact, throughout the years, I can't remember a single time they mentioned something I had done in the past that disappointed them. Once the situation was dealt with, it was as though it never happened. I don't recall my parents insisting I say "I'm sorry." Their forgiveness never rested on my recognition of my need for it.

Awareness of the blessing of forgiveness came to me as an adult. When I torment myself by thinking back to the things I've done, wishing I'd obeyed more, listened more, appreciated more, it isn't because my parents required some kind of penance. In fact, while at times I have wanted to sit with my parents and tell them "I'm sorry" for various things I did throughout my life, I have also realized they haven't wanted that.

My father died some years ago, but my mother is still forgiving. Because of their forgiveness I have been allowed to embrace life without looking back in shame.

One of my favorite Bible verses is Psalm 103:12. "As far as the east is from the west, so far does he remove our transgressions from us." The assurance I gain from this verse is the reality that my sin is removed so far from me that it cannot return to me or touch me. Because of God's forgiveness in Christ, my sin is as though it never existed. The legacy of forgiveness is a gift of God, and when we are fortunate to experience this gift in our parents, we find it easier to believe that the Lord can also forgive us.

Throughout the years I have met many people with deeply embedded grievances within their family. When adult children avoid their parents, or brothers and sisters have no contact for years, a long-held grudge must surely leave an enormous void that cries to be filled.

As I've observed my parents' response to issues within their extended families, they didn't allow their hurt to destroy the relationships. Throughout our lives, my sister and I have been encouraged to care about and be involved with our extended family. No matter how far we might live from other family members we reach out to celebrate and comfort one another.

Forgiveness is not a natural response to the wounds we receive from others. I'm sure my parents struggled with the decision to forgive at times. No doubt this was a decision they made again and again, not just once. And no doubt there were times when forgiving was much harder than at other times. Yet, their legacy of consistency in forgiving has allowed me to look at the situations I have faced and know that forgiveness is a valid option.

Forgiveness ushers in a long list of positive outcomes, including better health, peace of mind, ongoing relationships, trust, hope, and the list goes on. I can't think of a time I chose to forgive that I wish I had held a grudge. Forgiving others is one of the most freeing decisions of life, freeing everyone involved to the abundant life available in Christ.

The forgiveness I have received is a legacy I pray I am passing on to my daughter and grandchildren. I pray it will always be my response to my husband, my family, my friends, and my coworkers. Only in forgiving will we know the joy and peace Christ came to give.

ANDREA MULLINS is publisher for New Hope Publishers™ and directs World Crafts SM. Both are divisions of WMU®. She is a graduate of the University of Wyoming and holds a Master of Divinity from New Orleans Baptist Theological Seminary as well as a Doctor of Ministry from Bakke Graduate University. She is married to Mike and they have one married daughter and three grandchildren.

Can I Help?

For we are His workmanship, created in Christ Jesus for good works, which God prepared beforehand that we should walk in them.

(Ephesians 2:10, NKJV)

I think I've made a million cookies in my lifetime. Okay, at least thousands. I can picture them all lined up in rows. Sugar cookies. Almond praline. Magic cookie bars. Peanut Butter. Oatmeal Raisin. Chocolate chip …and so many more.

As a little girl, whenever I saw the flour, sugar, and vanilla come out of the cupboard, I was sure the baker needed my help, and I was ready to offer it. So I'd approach my mom. "Can I help?"

Help I did. I poured, cracked, and stirred. I snuck chocolate chips and licks off the mixers. I spooned batter onto trays and stood back to admire my work. Somehow, the flour dusting every surface went unnoticed to me. The eggshells I'd dropped on the floor and then stepped on, weren't even on my radar.

As I scampered off to play once the cookie sheets were in the oven, I had no idea that Mom would spend the next thirty minutes putting the kitchen back in order. As a mom of six *helpers,* I can imagine that she'd have sighed a few times. She might have wondered why she hadn't just waited until naptime.

A little while later, the timer would ding, and I'd run back into the almost spotless kitchen just in time to see my creation make its debut as Mom slid the tray out of the oven.

Cookies ran together. Tiny ones were burned around the edges, fat ones hadn't cooked all the way through. Yet, I saw a masterpiece, because that's what reflected back to me in my mother's eyes.

I lived for that look of pride on Mom's face, as every child does. She said they were the best she'd ever seen, every single time. And, oh, the taste. Melt-in-her-mouth goodness.

With six *helpers* of my own, I've found myself on the other end of that process. I've asked myself the same questions I'm sure my Mom asked herself, and her mother before that. "Can't I just wait until naptime?"

Oh, it's an indisputable fact that the cookie-making process would result in far fewer messes and better cookies if it took place after bedtime. But there's something about a child's clumsy hands, the looks of concentration and confusion, the careful efforts to do well. These are building blocks of character. Not to mention the growth that comes from learning to follow directions and teamwork.

When those cookies are finished and that young baker gazes up at Mommy and says, "Look what I made!" The rewards far outweigh the costs. Though that child couldn't have done it alone, Mommy happily hands over full credit for a job well done.

So it is with our Heavenly Father. Couldn't He do what needed to be done in this world without our help? He would be far more effective and efficient if we got our messes of gossip, misunderstandings, selfishness, and pride out of the way of His projects.

Even still, when something needs to be done, He gets it set up and then steps back and waits for us to partner with Him. He waits for us to come running toward Him shouting, "Daddy, Daddy! Can I help?"

It's for our benefit that He lets us get our hands dirty in the cookie batter of life. He simply smiles when we feel like we've done well and waits until we aren't looking to pick out the eggshells.

I'm so thankful for my mother's patience. As a result, I've strived to be that kind of mom to my kids. I'm also grateful that my Heavenly Father has allowed me and my kids to add hundreds more cookies to His pile. He never waits until naptime.

NICOLE O'DELL is the mom of six--including a set of toddler triplets. The founder of ChooseNOW Ministries and the host of Teen Talk Radio, Nicole is also and the author of over a dozen YA books, including the popular Scenarios for Girls interactive fiction series and the Diamond Estates Series. She also writes non-fiction for both teens and parents focusing on bridging the communication gap in preparation for life's tough choices. She can be found at www.nicoleodell.com.

Pearls of Selflessness

When I first became a mom, I didn't worry about if I would be able to take care of my baby. After all, I assumed I knew all the basics like changing diapers and making bottles from playing pretend with my baby dolls and mimicking my mom.

Instead, I grew anxious thinking about the bigger picture of it all. How in the world would I be able to give so much of myself to a child without being selfish? How do moms manage the entire house with children?

I didn't have to look too far for a great example. However, that didn't relieve my personal doubt. Since having such a great example in my mom, I worried if I'd be able to be just like her-- a gracefully selfless mom. That was my dilemma.

Before marriage and kids, I was used to living on my own and pursuing my own dreams and ambitions. I never really examined the idea of family and children. And even after I was married, I never considered the real responsibility of motherhood until the day my doctor placed my first child in my arms. That day, my nerves spiraled into a crazy web of anxiety.

I called my mom every single day. Most times, she could hear stress buzzing from the other end of the phone.

"Mom, the baby was up all last night, I just don't have any energy to do this."

"Mom, I don't have any time to cook dinner."

"Mom, I can't figure out how to balance it all."

"Mom, the baby's crying. I don't think he likes me!"

My complaints were pretty consistent and I'm sure very entertaining to my mom. Sometimes she'd laugh and say, "Kennisha, welcome to motherhood!"

Instead of encouraging my rants, she encouraged me to lean on the Lord. Instead of giving me sympathy, she prayed that God would give me wisdom. I often stood in awe of how my mom managed to watch a house full of children—ten toddlers—while still managing her household. And my mom did more than babysit them. She taught, trained and thoroughly enjoyed the ministry of keeping children during the day. She taught them scripture verses, important lessons on how to be loving and respectful to their parents. She danced, sang and built towers with them. And when they napped, she cleaned the house and cooked dinner before my father came home from work.

I've always thought of my mom as the Proverbs 31 woman. How accurately those verses describe her. But what amazes me is how she doesn't give herself much credit at all for keeping it all together. I recently asked her, "Mom, how did you do it all? How did you raise all of those children, plus your own, keep a clean house, feed us and make sure we were alright?"

Her answer: "He gives power to the weak and strength to the powerless." (Isaiah 40:29)

She went on to explain, "As moms, we feel overwhelmed and exhausted, with every stage motherhood has to bring. But there's one thing we should all never forget. It's that God gives us the strength and ability to do what we have to do for our families. He is the source of our strength and the strength of our life. It is only by the grace of God."

My mother consistently reminds me to align life properly with the word of God. I've learned that if I trust in the Lord with all of my heart, lean into his understanding and acknowledge him, that he'll direct my paths—even along this journey in motherhood.

That's exactly what helped her raise her children and pour into many others' lives. I'm thankful to have a mom who has shown me the true beauty of motherhood and how to selflessly embrace the calling.

KENNISHA HILL pens words of grace and hope through fiction and non-fiction books, including her latest memoir Once Upon A Child. You can spot occasional freelance articles from her in Relevant Magazine and various Christian-based magazines. She shares inspirational words weekly at her blog A Cup of Grace for Women and is a blogger for MomLife Today-- a division of Family Life. Visit her website at www.kennishahill.com

SARAH CHAPMAN MCMANUS

Whisper in the Night

I wanted to be a mom for as long as I can remember, but my journey got off to a rocky start. I was barely home from the hospital with our long awaited, treasured daughter, when I wanted to take her right back. The problem was me. She deserved the best mother ever, and I knew that couldn't be me.

Oh, I'd made a good attempt to get ready to be a good mom. I read lots of books. I paid close attention in the hospital's parenting classes. I spent a lot of time and effort putting together an awesome nursery.

My husband and I picked just the right furniture, a gorgeous set with a safe, comfy crib, a good sized chest, and, of course, the very important changing table. I covered one wall with a colorful jungle print fabric and even cut out and painted balsa wood animals to make a fantastic carousel lamp. Everything was ready and so cute.

But in spite of all my careful preparation, I was alone in the middle of the night, unable to calm one tiny baby. I fed her and changed her. I rocked her and sang to her. Yet, she cried. I cried. What was wrong with her? Was she sick? What was wrong with me?

As a professional I was a fairly confident, competent person. I could write policies and procedures. I could meet goals and standards. I could evaluate and teach. What happened?

Nothing prepared me for the reality of being responsible for the very life of another human being. And if I couldn't cope now, how would I handle even harder things in the future? I despaired in that dark night.

I didn't think to cry out to God. But I remembered a hospital nurse saying, "If you have any questions, just call, day or night. We're up anyway."

Did she mean it? I hoped so, since there was no one else I felt I could disturb in the middle of the night. And somehow darkness seemed to multiply my fears.

A kind stranger's voice reassured me. My baby was fine. Normal. I was doing fine, too. Everything would be okay.

God bless that nurse. It was her voice I heard, but I felt God's whisper in my heart. Hope and peace replaced my fear.

Of course, that night long ago was not the last time I felt fear for my children. Nor was it the last time I felt inadequate. Motherhood is not a destination, but a journey. A long journey.

God has promised to never leave me, never to abandon me in any trouble, and he always keeps his promises. One promise in the Bible says, "The Lord himself goes before you and will be with you; he will never leave you nor forsake you. Do not be afraid; do not be discouraged." (Deuteronomy 31:8, TNIV)

It's a theme repeated through the Bible: *Fear not because God is there.* Not only is he always with me, but he sends others to help me, sometimes unseen angels, sometimes kind strangers or family or friends.

Through bumps and bruises and burns. Through coughs and croup and convulsions. Through dating and drivers ed and even disheartening silence. I am never alone in my journey even through my darkest night.

Motherhood is like a thrilling, lifetime rollercoaster ride. There are

SARAH CHAPMAN MCMANUS writes, teaches, and speaks at women's events encouraging and equipping people to live life to the max. A few of Sarah's favorite things are food, fun, and her fantasy of catching up on her to-do list someday. Sarah and her husband David travel frequently since her most favorite thing is spending time with family and friends. www.SarahChapman McManus.com frequent up, up, ups and some downs, too. Snuggly baby hugs. Smart teenage sass. It doesn't come with many awards, but lots of rewards. And my favorite reward so far? Watching my daughter laughing, loving, hugging, kissing, being the best mom ever to her own child.

DAWN MEEHAN

Having Patience with Pink-Dog Days

I walked into the kitchen and froze in my tracks. Glancing down, I discovered I was standing in an inch of soapy water. Before I could ascertain where the water was coming from, my son slid by me, skidding barefoot through the slippery mess. My eyes followed him as he hydroplaned through the kitchen and disappeared down the long hallway. No sooner did he slide out of sight, than my daughter flew toward me from the opposite direction.

"This is so much fun! Try it, Mom!" My kids cheered as they slid around the kitchen. They sounded so innocent, like it had never occurred to them that it was a bad idea to cover the floor in water and dish soap.

Looking back, I think I probably should've joined them in their fun. At the time, however, I think my head actually exploded as I yelled, "What on earth were you thinking? Why did you pour water and soap on the floor?"

Then there was the time my two youngest children filled the bathroom sink with water, shampoo, toothpaste and earthworms. They used my toothbrush to stir their potion. If I recall, my exact words to them were, "What were you thinking? Why are there worms in the sink? My toothbrush???" I'm pretty sure they answered my shouts with a well-thought-out, "I dunno."

And who could forget the time they tried to flush Barbie and her friends down the toilet? Although the commode may look like a fun whirlpool for the dolls, my hefty plumbing bill says otherwise.

Over the years, my kids have given each other impromptu haircuts (did you know that one-inch bangs don't look good on anyone?). They've decorated the walls and the furniture with works of art rendered in permanent marker, and they've jumped off the top bunk, breaking bones as they landed. A number large enough to count the messes they've made over the years hasn't been invented.

Not only have they made many questionable decisions, but I've given up all hope of the kids ever learning how to replace the empty roll of toilet paper. I'd be shocked speechless if they figured out how to hang up their coats, put their clean folded laundry in their dressers, or take off their socks without turning them into wadded-up balls.

With six kids, we've certainly had our share of adventures and mishaps. Sometimes it seems as if I've failed this whole parenting thing. I continuously teach them right from wrong and try to instill a good set of morals. I attempt to get them to think before acting, and to make wise decisions. And yet, they continue to do things like paint the dog pink, shove candy up their noses, and jump off the garage roof. Sometimes I want to throw my hands up in the air and shout, "I give up!"

And then I think of our father, our heavenly father. How many times has He told us not to do something, only to watch us turn around and do it anyway? How many times has He instructed us on how we're to behave, only to have us do the opposite of what He says? How many times has He forgiven us, only to have us immediately make the same mistake

After Dawn auctioned a pack of Pokemon cards on eBay, she attracted the attention of nearly a hundred thousand readers in one day. Her blog, BecauseISaidSo.com skyrocketed to become one of the most popular mommy blogs on the net. In 2008, her blog was voted the Best Parenting Blog by The Blogger's Choice Awards. It was also nominated for the Best Humor Blog, the Hottest Mommy Blogger, and the Best Blog of All Time.

again? If I were God, I'd want to throw my hands up in the air and shout, "I give up!"

But thankfully, He doesn't. He forgives endlessly. He teaches always. He's there for us when we mess up time and time again. It somehow makes it a little easier to forgive, and it reminds me not to give up on this parenting thing. Although I'm pretty sure they'll never learn how to replace the empty toilet paper roll. I've definitely given up there.

Standing in the Gap

It was on a cool, crisp Saturday morning, a perfect day for football. Our oldest son was about the age of eleven and holding down his position on the line. He and his teammates looked so much like men gone off to war as they ran up and down the football field chasing the pigskin. I watched the game while keeping an eye on our younger toddler.

I must admit, I'm a fair-weather football fan. I've never been too excited about twenty-two kids tackling and crashing into one another. Our team had established a comfortable lead when my husband, the head coach, decided to put our son in the position of quarterback. I wasn't too keen on this strategic move either. I picked up our toddler and placed him on my hip so I could engage in the game. Our oldest son was out on the field, calling and executing the plays.

During the next play, as my son looked for someone to receive his pass, a kid on the other team had the audacity to sack my child. The ball was fumbled, causing both teams to heap up in a huge pile atop of my son in order to retrieve the ball. They scrambled hard until the play was over. When the dust settled, everyone got up except for my son. He laid there motionless.

My husband and all of the other coaches rushed onto the field as onlookers held their breath. I could hear my husband's urgent requests, "Come on, son. Talk to me – you can do it."

My son did not respond.

In a moment of desperation, I asked a friend to hold the baby. With the determination of a mother bear looking after her cub, I headed for the thirty yard line. My husband and I had been married long enough to establish that silent, non-verbal communication we had read so much about. He looked me dead in the eye as if to say, "Don't even think about coming out here on this field." I eyeballed him back as if to say, "Baby, I love you, but you and all your friends have experimented long enough. It's time for you all to step aside. Mama is coming on the field and Mama means business."

My husband and all the coaches all parted like the Red Sea to let me through.

I got down in the dirt upon that muddy field and I laid hands upon my son. I prayed aloud, "In the name of Jesus, rise up off of this field and walk again!" Before I could say, 'Amen,' I heard my son call my name. He said, " Mama? *Mama, get off the field!*"

After this episode, my husband and son were so embarrassed that they threatened to banish me, begging me never to show my face at the park again. I asked their forgiveness, but assured them that as a mom, I'd run out on the field all over again if necessary.

Sometimes life is like that. God calls us to bear one another's burdens— to minister to the lost, the hurting and the next generation, just as Jesus did. Isaiah 61:1-2 gives us our directive.

"The spirit of the Lord is upon me; because the Lord hath anointed me to preach good

BABBIE MASON is a Dove Award-winning and Grammy nominated gospel singer, songwriter, author, creator of the Embrace: A Worship Event for Women ministry, professor of songwriting at Atlanta Christian College and Lee University, and a television talk-show host. She was inducted into the Christian Music Hall of Fame in 2010 and has appeared on numerous national television and radio programs. Babbie has been honored perform for Presidents Gerald Ford, Jimmy Carter, George H. W. Bush, George W. Bush, Lady Margaret Thatcher, Colin Powell, Steve Forbes among many others. Babbie performs a holiday special at Carnegie Hall every year. Babbie lives near Atlanta on a farm with her husband Charles.

tidings to the meek, he hath sent me to bind up the brokenhearted, to proclaim liberty to the captives, and the opening of the prison to them that are bound." (KJV)

Sure enough, there are those who are down and out on the street where you live; somebody within a few doors is fighting a relentless battle with cancer. Someone's marriage is in trouble. Someone's child is on drugs. The hungry, hopeless and hurting are probably not too far from where you are right now.

Wherever you are compelled to serve, pray and ask God to feed the hungry, to clothe the naked, to spread the gospel around your city and around the world, to heal the sick and encourage the downtrodden. Ask Him to use you to help Him accomplish this great mission.

The Queen of Everything

I am often told that I am the queen of over-commitment, trying to pack more into a day than most normal people would fit into a week. This is a gift I received my mother.

My mother, Barbara Snyders, is one of those people who cannot say no to someone in need—to a family member, a friend, or a complete stranger. My entire life, I watched her spend countless hours helping others. As a teacher, she helped kindergartners learn how to tie their shoes and taught high school students geometry, algebra and physics. If there was a student struggling socially or academically, she gave them caring support. When my eight-year-old cousin needed a new home, she took him in and raised him like her own. She gave him a life he never would have had. She engaged my siblings and me in music, sports and academics, driving us to succeed.

All of this is amazing in and of itself, but there is something that makes my mother even more special. At the age of eight, she was struck with polio. She spent months in the hospital away from her parents. With no mommy to comfort her (parents were not allowed to stay), she endured the painful treatments and therapies alone. She survived, but her right arm was rendered useless. She learned to write again with her left hand. She learned to tie her shoes with one hand. She earned valedictorian of her high school class and followed that feat with eight years of college while raising four babies. She taught kindergartners how to tie their shoes even though she only had one hand. She played baseball, holding the bat under her bad arm, throwing the ball up in the air with her good arm and then pulling the bat out to hit the ball as it came back down. It was so impressive to watch her. She could do things with one hand that most people could not do with two.

More than anything, my mother taught me to never give up. When I was thirteen years old, our house burned to the ground as we watched. Everything that she and my father had worked for was gone in a matter of hours. We started over with nothing but the clothes on our backs. My sister and I were sharing a babysitting job that summer. As my mother taught us, we did not let the family down. The next morning after the fire, while we were staying with friends, I got up and walked to the babysitting job. I did not have any shoes, so I walked there bare-footed to do my shift.

• • • • • • • • • • • • • • • • • • • •

REBECCA DARR is the Executive Director of WINGS (Women In Need Growing Stronger) in the Chicago area. WINGS provides resources and emergency housing for women and their children facing homelessness. In addition, WINGS 15,000 square foot Safe House can accommodate up to 45 women and children each night. WINGS programs include Project Lifeline, a graduate mentoring service, children's activities, homeless prevention and resources options and Career Services. For more info visit www.wingsprogram.com.

Because my mother had helped so many people, our church congregation and many others in the community took up collections of money and clothes to help us. It was such a difficult time for all of us, but we stuck together and grew stronger as a family. Like so many times before in her life, my mother persevered to better times. Thanks to her, my siblings and I have been blessed with many. Her faith in God carried her through those times of grit to transform them into pearls. I am eternally grateful for her legacy of faith, commitment and perseverance.

Mrs Brady She Was Not

I wished my mother was Mrs. Brady.

But she could not have been more different.

Not till I was an adult did I accept that Mrs. Brady was a well-scripted TV "dream mother" that met the ideals of many like myself. My mother, however, was real. Sadly, the memory bank of the petulant little child in me focused on what I did not get.

However, one of the lovely riches of adulthood is to be able to reflect on one's memories of childhood and in lucky circumstances, to be able to recalibrate, each time letting the stored anger be released.

Unlike Mrs. Brady, my mother was a stoic figure with few words. She was a disciplinarian and believed in punishment when we misbehaved. I yearned for a mother who cuddled and praised when praise was due. I wanted her encouragement, to give me strength and the confidence to be more.

Instead, unbeknownst to me then, her tactic, alongside many other ancient Chinese approaches to child rearing, was "negative reinforcement." That was her way to ensure that I would not be complacent, and always try to be better.

Being the middle of three girls, I thought of myself as Jan Brady. So it seemed appropriate that I was "difficult" and my mother bewildered over how to deal with this demanding child who had far-flung ideas of grandeur.

As soon as I could, I took flight and eagerly left Malaysia, my home and my parents. I went to further my education in New York and search for my Brady Bunch dream. Ironically, I now realize that my parents afforded me the means to move away from the life they gave me.

As much of a disciplinarian as my mother was, she did not even attempt to clip my wings. Instead she did cut the apron strings and let me go. I'm sure at times she was afraid for me, but I also now know that, as humble as she was in her life, she was immensely proud of me from a distance – where I kept her.

Time passes by all too quickly and often we are caught unaware.

A stroke left my mother partially incapacitated. I did not make it back in time before she suffered a second stroke that left her on life support. When I finally entered the hospital room where my mother lay, her eyes were closed shut. Her chest rose and fell as if she was sound asleep. But she was comatose.

I felt the strangeness of seeing the strong woman I thought I knew, lying still and lifeless. A few years after and much later in life, I finally gave thought to who my mother might have been.

As I tried to piece together the stories of her early years, I began to let go of the "dragon mother" image I had of her. Lurking at the back of my mind were two heart-to-heart conversations we had many, many years ago.

I was, as usual, asking for something extravagant that was beyond the family's means. I heard the same old response—how she and my father worked hard and saved to make ends meet, that we must focus on doing well in school and not be distracted with frivolous things.

At both those times, she spoke longingly of the love she had yearned for from her parents. Instead of that tyrant of a disciplinarian, I caught a glimpse of a vulnerable woman.

My mother was the second in a family of seven, and the eldest girl. When my grandfather and her oldest brother both died in the war, my grandmother was left to raise the family. As soon as my mother could, she worked to help support her younger siblings and became responsible for the family's financial wellbeing. She never had a chance to enjoy life's pleasure.

My mother was thrifty, but not just because her family lived through the war. She and my father wanted to be sure they could afford her daughters a roof over their head and an education. She sacrificed any notion of self-indulgence for her children.

When circumstances eventually allowed me to get off the fast paced treadmill, I was given an opportunity to recognize and reflect on the anger I held against my parents. The problem was that the little child I had been did not see nor understand an unglamourous aspect of love.

I am saddened that I never gave our mother-daughter relationship a chance when she was alive. But there is no time to dwell on mistakes made in youth. As a consolation I now use that strong willed determination she passed onto me—to try every day to be a better me than I was yesterday.

MAY PING WONG was born in Malaysia. She attended university in New York City and attained an international MBA at the University of South Carolina. She began her career in advertising in New York, then pursued it further in Dusseldorf, Milan and Hong Kong. In 1994 she moved to England and has since made London her home. She returned to NYC and after seven successful years in marketing luxury real estate she jumped off the corporate treadmill to "smell the roses" and "do all the things she had wanted to do. May now resides in London and continues her passion for interior decorating whilst experimenting with new ideas and working on her writing.

JULIE PAPIEVIS

●

A Message From My Grandmothers

We are often given advice from previous generations as we pass through life, but most times we may not feel inclined to heed or even hear it. There are also those times when we cannot possibly ignore the messages that we may receive, because of where and how we receive them.

I feel inextricably drawn to the message from my grandmothers, because of how and where I received it. I was involved in a serious, life-threatening car crash in which a young man was speeding, ran a red light and hit my sports car broad-side, which sent it rolling backwards and the force of the impact twisting my head and neck so severely, it came within two millimeters of severing my brainstem. As my neurosurgeon says, "we live in our brainstems," and as mine was so badly damaged, my body began dying. Our Lord intervened, putting an off-duty paramedic and doctor at the scene, who immediately lifted my head and started an airway and called 911. When the paramedics arrived only 2 minutes later, it was obvious that there was nothing to do but to get me to the closest trauma center immediately.

In the ambulance, on the way to the trauma center, my body began to complete the dying process, where I had begun agonal breathing—or our "last breaths." My body had released all of the remaining fluid, completing the dying process. The paramedics arriving at the scene to dropping me off at the trauma center took only fourteen minutes. The paramedics call ahead to prepare the trauma center for any person and situation they are bringing, and they had done so in my case. A world renowned neurosurgeon was waiting when I arrived. The paramedics never called to check on how I was doing, as they "knew" that I would not live.

The first test that was administered to me at the trauma center, given the nature of my injury, was an EEG, to measure the relative brain function in my body. There was a base-line or no response. Given the extent of my injuries, the mortality rate for my injury is 96%. The remaining 4% usually die within six months due to complications, and the very few remaining are semi-vegetative, being toileted and fed in a nursing facility.

Forward to over a month later, and I'm waking up from my coma. Paralyzed, unable to speak, see or swallow, that's when I remembered the message from my grandmothers. That's when I remembered that I had died.

I was in an area of all light. No floors or ceilings. No corners-everything was round-except there was a long, narrow aisle way to my left that I was drawn to go towards/through. This was a place of perfect peace. I knew that I was there because I was dead. I was happy to be there. I wanted to stay, but I realized I wasn't alone. So I suddenly was in front of my two deceased grandmothers. They told me that I could not stay--that I had to go back. I said, "I can't

After a horrific car accident sent her to the gates of heaven and back, JULIE PAPIEVIS had, at best, a four percent chance of survival, rating a "3", the lowest number possible on the Glascow Coma Scale. The few who survive typically face a non-functional life. She, however, completely beat the odds even though she remained in a coma for over a month. Today, Julie has a national speaking and lecturing career as a survivor of traumatic brain stem injury. She has appeared on The 700 Club, CNN, WGN News and many others. She has also been featured in First for Women Magazine, The Chicago Tribune, Woman's Day Magazine, and Lifetime TV's "Beyond Chance" to share her story. She is based in the Chicago area. Julie is an advocate for other survivors looking for hope and guidance. www.gobackandbehappy.com

go back. I'm not physically okay." I pointed to my left side that was paralyzed.

My grandmother said, "Your body will heal. Go back and be happy."

Words to live by. Those words are my first memory after waking from my month-long coma in a completely disabled state. Those words were what I heard while taking my last lap of my triathlon fourteen years later.

"Your body will heal. Go back and be happy."

Becoming a Mother of Pearl

In Hollywood circles, I am known as a Mama Bear—always very protective of my children and of the people who God places in my life. On the movie sets, I constantly pray for and with the actors, their families, the directors, and for everyone who is involved in each part of the production process. As we "take five" on the set, I make a point to talk with the cast and crew. Over a cup of coffee, many of them have shared their difficulties and have asked for prayer.

Throughout the years, God has taught me an important lesson and life skill: Listening. Yes, listening is one of the greatest gifts a mother can give to her child and that we can give to others. Sometimes talking is so much easier to do than listening, isn't it? However, listening is a manifestation of love, and it's a cornerstone of building a strong relationship – including a solid relationship with God.

Learning to be still so we can know God and listen to Him can be a huge challenge within the demands of our daily schedules. However, when we hear His words and heed His promptings, we have the incredible honor and opportunity of becoming a Mother of Pearl—a manifestation of God's grace and love.

I have always loved the beauty and significance of pearls. The Biblical "pearl of great price" is Christ. His sacrificial blood is the nacre that covers the grit of our sins, transforming us from sinners into saints so we can enjoy a relationship with God.

I love to wear pearls. To me, a pearl necklace isn't just a beautiful piece of jewelry; it's a tangible reminder of God's grace. As with any of my material possessions, I know that everything belongs to Him. I am merely a temporary steward. I never anticipated that my pearls would become a ministry.

One day while I was at a bank, the teller admired my pearl necklace. "My pearls just broke," she said. At that moment, God spoke to my heart: "Lani, these pearls you are wearing are hers."

I took off my necklace and handed it to the young woman. "I'd like to give you mine. The Lord wants you to have these beautiful pearls because He knows your needs and loves you so much."

She was stunned as tears welled in her eyes. "Thank you," she said with an overflowing heart. "What you don't know is that I was in a car wreck and just lost everything."

One day, I was wearing an opera length set of pearls while I was speaking with a pastor's wife. "Those are her pearls you are wearing," God directed. I removed the two strands from my neck and gave them to this woman. She told me she had been crying all morning wondering if God even noticed her.

By hearing God and heeding His promptings, we can reach out to strangers and bless them with words or actions. The best gift a Mother of Pearl can give is a "hug from heaven."

In an industry rampant with temptation and excess, **LANI NETTER** has maintained her Christian morals and values. Lani is married to Gil Netter, Hollywood Producer of 26 feature films such as Academy Award Winner, The Blind Side, Marley and Me, and Flicka. While living the role of a Hollywood wife, she devoted herself to her two children; Jake, 23 and Grace, 15. Lani started her own values-based production company. She currently has one film and two documentaries in production, all of which have a core essence of God's message. She is also on the Advisory Film Board at Pepperdine University. Two charities that she champions are The Union Rescue Mission and The Dream Center. www.laniinc.com/

KAREN O'CONNOR

Mother Knows Best

My mother enjoyed reminding me of the popular phrase, "Mother Knows Best." She didn't always say it in words, but she made her point, from setting bedtimes when I was a child to establishing curfews when I was a teenager. Thanks to Mom––who was also my Girl Scout leader––I developed a yen for hiking, flower-gazing, and camp weekends where I tromped through the creek and spent quiet moments sitting in the crook of a tree.

She also infused in me a love of words. "I'm a word-person," she'd say as she worked the crossword puzzle in the daily newspaper. My car license plate, WORDY, speaks of my love affair with words to this day.

One October afternoon in 2003, my sister called to tell me that Mom had passed away in her sleep in the nursing home where she'd spent her last five years. The news rocked my world. It didn't matter that Mom was eighty-nine years old when she died and that she'd "lived a good long life," as friends are eager to remind one at such a time. Eva O'Connor was *my* mother and *my* life changed the moment she was gone. I would not hear her voice again nor feel the touch of her hand on mine.

Later, my siblings and I gathered at the mortuary to say our last good-bye before cremation. I looked at Mother's body nestled in the simple cardboard box, the soft wisps of gray hair that framed her peaceful face, and the clean white bed sheet that swaddled her body. I clutched my brother's arm and he placed his right hand over my trembling one.

We stepped back and the mortician replaced the top of the box, and then signaled the assistant to ignite the furnace. Whoosh! The flames leapt from the burner as the mortician wheeled the table to the entrance of the chamber and slid the container into the vault. I watched in awe as the tongues of fire licked the sides of the box. Tears ran down my face, my legs wobbled, and my heart raced at the sight of my mother returning to dust before my very eyes.

> *"...For dust you are and to dust you will return."*
> *(Genesis 3:19, NIV)*

What had once been my mother's body––the one that had given birth to me––would soon be contained in a small bronze urn. I peered through the small window of the vault and wiped my eyes. Then we turned and walked out of that cold room, down the steps, and into the warm October sunshine.

I lifted my heart in a silent prayer of thanksgiving for my mother, for all she had meant to me and for all she had done for me—from coaching me before a spelling bee to listening to me practice before a piano recital. She had comforted me when I lost a best friend and encouraged me when I married and moved far away. She was at my side when I gave birth to my children, and she was there on the dark day when my first marriage ended.

Eva O'Connor had not been a perfect mother. But she had been the perfect mother *for me*. I closed my eyes for a moment as I lingered over the memory of her.

Then slowly a small bubble of joy worked its way up from my toes to my lips. "Praise you, O God," I shouted within. "You have been Mother's Lord all the days of her life, even to her old age and gray hair. And now you have carried her into Paradise."

My mourning turned to joy in that moment––at a most unexpected time in a most unexpected place.

KAREN O'CONNOR is an award-winning author of more than seventy books and hundreds of magazine pieces. For more information, please visit Karen's website: www.karenoconnor.com.

Little Letters of Love

My mom never claimed to be perfect. In fact, she allowed me the privilege of seeing her mistakes.

Like many girls, the teenage years were the most difficult on my relationship with my mother. Our emotions got the best of us sometimes. My mom would be the first to say she was not the perfect parent; but slammed doors, temper tantrums, and long, silent grudges were common ways I dealt with the ups and downs of the growing up years.

Now that my husband and I are ready to start a family, I have to admit, once again, that I will never be perfect. I am still known for sometimes stomping up the stairs when I'm angry, shouting hurtful words, and finding it difficult to forgive. But I so desperately want to be a strong mother, who never cries, never yells at my children, or never fights with my husband in front of them. I want to have it all together before I become a mother. Free from mistakes and failures.

Perfect.

However, I am learning to pry off perfection's cruel grip on my heart.

In the face of my own mother, I see beauty personified in her imperfections. She didn't hide her heart from me. She revealed herself, sometimes regretfully, other times courageously. My mom and dad had a real marriage. They argued. I remember her going on drives to relieve her frustrations. I remember her tears. But that's okay.

Because what I remember most is how she taught me to seek restoration quickly.

Although I wasn't always ready to start talking, my mom would hurry up to my room to admit her mistakes if we had just fought. Usually it was more quickly than I liked. I wanted time to think about how right I was and how wrong she was. Usually she would just have to apologize for raising her voice, while I had to confess my bad attitude, disobedience, and hateful words.

On more than once occasion, my mom would tuck little notes into my bedroom. Restoration notes. She would tell me she was sorry if she hurt me, and finish with words of love and affirmation. Words she penned as an effort to help me see that although I had messed up, she also had a part to play.

She doesn't know it, but they left a mark on my heart forever. Ninety-nine percent of the time, I was the one who normally caused the fight and did the most damage. Nevertheless, my mom always let me know when she too was guilty.

I know many mothers who try desperately to play the part. Underneath their well-placed hair, flawless make-up, and sweet words is a wealth of imperfections, sins, failures, and secrets. They don't let anyone in, especially not their children. They try to hold themselves together. However, in doing so, they give their children only a part of who they are, not their whole heart. Without realizing it, they can encourage their children walk through life with walls.

My mom's notes left imprints of the Savior's perfection on my heart. God always gives second chances. He never withholds his love, even in my sin. True, my mom's restoration notes honestly exposed her faults, but even more importantly, they unveiled the forgiveness of my Heavenly Father.

They led me to the original writer of restoration…Jesus.

As a mother, you never have to worry that your shortcomings will

CHARISSA STEYN is a writer, counselor, speaker, and blogger living in South Africa with her husband. Find out more by visiting her blog, Everyday Adventures at CharSteyn.blogspot.com.

disqualify you from such a divine calling. Live honestly and openly before your children, placing your imperfections at His feet, and seek His restoration every day in your relationships...through your words, actions, and yes, even little letters. *This is love.*

The Safe House

When I hear the word "ex-con," I envision a big, burly guy who uses salty language with a smooth delivery. The antithesis of this description is: a petite gal, who only uses God's name in praise, and is no "smooth-talker." I've just described Cindy, mother of three and former inmate. She shattered my stereotype.

Cindy's story will floor you. It did me. We met two years ago, when she joined the leadership team at a bible study in which I also am involved. She would matter-of-factly say something like, "When I was in jail..." as casually as I may say, "When I was in the bookstore..." With Cindy, these days, there are no more secrets.

Secrets have a way of seeping out until they are fully exposed. Alcohol addiction was the secret Cindy kept. Fear of rejection and the desire to portray the image of perfection permeated her life. With the illusion of a happy family came invisible shame. Although the alcoholism had not yet been revealed, its affects were evident. Rage and legalism ran the house. From an onlooker's perspective, her life appeared to be flawless. But...nothing was further from the truth.

Cindy was in a downward spiral. She had discovered her husband's addiction to pornography. She was the caretaker for her dying mother. And her oldest child had just attempted suicide. She turned to alcohol, her companion twenty years earlier, because it numbed the pain. She began drinking heavily.

One evening she got behind the wheel when inebriated. As Cindy tells it, "God told me he loved me too much to let me go down this path. In his severe mercy he allowed me to be pulled over and arrested. This was the biggest gift God could have given me and my family."

Cindy was sentenced to six months in prison. She was faced with a choice: to fight or to surrender. She chose surrender and to cling to God. In her heart of hearts, she wanted to be a good mom and wife. She prayed her family would remain intact. I don't know about you, but I would have thrown in the towel and said, "Enough!" But God continued to work in Cindy and through her situation as she relied on him.

While incarcerated, she dealt with her alcoholism and her husband addressed his porn addiction. Relationships within the family slowly began to heal. Honesty replaced deception. There were lots of tears and difficult conversations. Because she was removed from the home, she was not able to be the buffer between the kids and their dad. The four of them had to figure out how to effectively interact with each other, even when angry. Another blessing.

Her daughter, being the oldest, had the deepest wounds. It has been three years since Cindy was released and the healing continues to take place. Through the heartache they have done a lot of soul searching and relational work. Counseling plus praying together daily has positively impacted the entire family.

The kids are free to discuss anything and everything. Cindy says, "It's easier for the kids to be honest with me and with my husband because the two of us have been so open about our brokenness." Once your weaknesses and sinfulness are revealed, you end up being an incredible safe person with whom to share intimate things.

The whole experience has drastically changed how her entire family relates to one another. Although things are not perfect (and they never will be this side of heaven), peace, joy, forgiveness, openness, and truthfulness fill the home. The underlying message is, "Do today well. But if you don't, let's talk about it and learn from it. We all make mistakes." Cindy's home is now a safe place to be real. No pretending allowed.

The verse that speaks to Cindy is, "Her many sins have been forgiven-for she loved much. But he who has been forgiven little loves little" (Luke 7: 47, NIV). Since she's been forgiven much, she loves big. She loves the Lord with all her heart, mind, and soul. The legacy she wants leave with her children is, "The truth will set you free" (John 8:32b NIV). She has been given a second chance. She hasn't just gone through rehabilitation, she has experienced transformation. God's love is powerful. My friend, Cindy, the ex-con, knows faith, family, and freedom are precious gifts from God. Her story helps me see life a little more clearly, too.

LORI WILDENBERG
Speaker, Licensed Parent and Family Educator, co-author of EMPOWERED PARENTS: Putting Faith First (Wildenberg & Danielson) lives in Colorado with her husband and four children. Visit her website www.loriwildenberg.com for more information.

A Word from the Charities
Supported by Pearl Girls®

WINGS

The proceeds from *Pearl Girls®: Encountering Grit, Experiencing Grace* helped WINGS to meet their mission of ending domestic violence and homelessness for hundreds of families. WINGS provides emergency and transitional housing to women and children fleeing domestic violence and homelessness. Families receive up to 2 years of support including counseling, career mentoring, financial assistance designed to move them from crisis to stability.

Proceeds from this book will go to support a new fund called 'Romeo's Fund' and will help hire a manager for the Safe House. March 15, 2011 would have been Romeo's 6th birthday, and in honor of his birth, his mother, a WINGS graduate and one of the first people to stay at WINGS Safe House domestic violence shelter, started Romeo's Fund. Romeo's birth and death were the reason his mother finally decided to get help for the abuse she was receiving at the hands of her husband. His beating caused the premature birth and ultimate death of her precious son and Romeo's mother knew she could no longer bear the abuse or its impact on her one and two year-old sons.

With the help of WINGS, Romeo's mother started on the road to a new life for herself and her children. She went back to school, received her degree, found employment and obtained counseling for the three of them. Her sons are now thriving in a loving home that she has made for them.

WINGS is honored by the support of Pearl Girls®.

HANDS OF HOPE

Hands of Hope wishes to thank Pearl Girls® for their generous contribution towards a well in Uganda. This well will continue to provide clean drinking water to over 600 children in Rahaama, Uganda for many years to come.

A Word of Thanks

How can I even begin to say "thank you" to the many wonderful women who have "tithed their talent" by sharing their stories for this special project. Thank you for sharing your gift!

And thank you to Amy Lathrop, a dear friend who patiently navigated this book through the many stages and who graciously guided me through the process. You are such a blessing!

Thank you Carl Raymond for opening the door to this generous opportunity to publish through Inspiring Voices. Thank you Lisa, Allan and the rest of the amazing team at Inspiring Voices for your patience, your professionalism and for your personal encouragement.

And a very special thank-you to my husband, David McSweeney who constantly supports my writing projects with love and patience. You are my soulmate! Also, thank you to my two precious daughters, Melissa and Katie. What an honor and joy to be your mother! Please forgive my many parenting mistakes and always remember that I love you!

And thank you, Lord for your constant grace, love and patience. May this book be a blessing to others and may the stories strengthen and encourage their faith and draw them closer to You. Please be especially close to the women and children who are seeking safe shelter through Wings and clean water through Hands of Hope.
Amen.